This book belongs to

Celebrate the Seasons

Content and Artwork by **Gooseberry Patch Company**

LEISURE ARTS
Vice President and Editor-in-Chief: Sandra Graham Case
Executive Director of Publications: Cheryl Nodine Gunnells
Director of Designer Relations: Debra Nettles
Publications Director: Kristine Anderson Mertes
Design Director: Cyndi Hansen
Editorial Director: Susan Frantz Wiles
Photography Director: Lori Ringwood Dimond
Art Operations Director: Jeff Curtis
Licensed Product Coordinator: Lisa Truxton Curton

EDITORIAL STAFF

EDITORIAL
Managing Editor: Alan Caudle
Senior Editor: Linda L. Garner
Associate Editor: Kimberly L. Ross

TECHNICAL
Managing Editor: Leslie Schick Gorrell
Book Coordinator and Senior Technical Writer:
    Theresa Hicks Young
Technical Writers: Jean W. Lewis, Christina Price Kirkendoll,
    and Shawnna B. Manes

FOODS
Foods Editor: Celia Fahr Harkey, R.D.
Technical Assistant: Judy Millard

DESIGN
Lead Designer: Diana Sanders Cates
Designers: Polly Tullis Browning, Cherece Athy,
    Peggy Elliott Cunningham, Anne Pulliam Stocks,
    Linda Diehl Tiano and Becky Werle
Craft Assistant: Lucy Beaudry

ART
Art Publications Director: Rhonda Hodge Shelby
Art Imaging Director: Mark Hawkins
Art Category Manager: Lora Puls
Graphic Artists: Dayle S. Cosh, Matt Davis, Rebecca J. Hester,
    and Elaine Wheat
Imaging Technician: Mark Potter
Staff Photographer: Russell Ganser
Staff Photography Stylists: Janna Laughlin and Cassie Newsome
Publishing Systems Administrator: Becky Riddle
Publishing Systems Assistants: Myra S. Means and
    Chris Wertenberger

PROMOTIONS
Associate Editor: Steven M. Cooper
Designer: Dale Rowett
Graphic Artist: Deborah Kelly

BUSINESS STAFF
Publisher: Rick Barton
Vice President, Finance: Tom Siebenmorgen
Director of Corporate Planning and Development:
    Laticia Mull Cornett
Vice President, Retail Marketing: Bob Humphrey
Vice President, Sales: Ray Shelgosh
Vice President, National Accounts: Pam Stebbins
Director of Sales and Services: Margaret Reinold
Vice President, Operations: Jim Dittrich
Comptroller, Operations: Rob Thieme
Retail Customer Service Managers: Sharon Hall and Stan Raynor
Print Production Manager: Fred F. Pruss

Library of Congress Catalog Number 2002113496
Hardcover ISBN 1-57486-278-2
Softcover ISBN 1-57486-279-0

10   9   8   7   6   5   4   3   2   1

Celebrate the Seasons

Welcome to Our Neighborhood

A LEISURE ARTS PUBLICATION

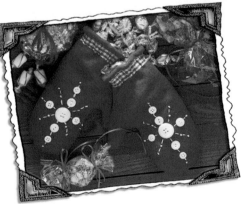

Four seasons fill the measure of the year. ~Keats

How Did Gooseberry Patch Get Started?

You may know the story of Gooseberry Patch...the tale of two country friends who decided one day over the backyard fence to try their hands at the mail order business. Started in JoAnn's kitchen back in 1984, Vickie & JoAnn's dream of a "Country Store in Your Mailbox" has grown and grown to a 96-page catalog with over 400 products, including cookie cutters, Santas, snowmen, gift baskets, angels and our very own line of cookbooks! What an adventure for two country friends!

Through our catalogs and books, Gooseberry Patch has met country friends from all over the world. While sharing letters and phone calls, we found that our friends love to cook, decorate, garden and craft. We've created Kate, Holly & Mary Elizabeth to represent these devoted friends who live and love the country lifestyle the way we do. They're just like you & me... they're our "Country Friends®!"

Your friends at Gooseberry Patch

A friend can touch your heart from across the world or across a room.

Through Summer, Winter, Spring & fall, Laugh & celebrate them all!

~KATE~

★Don't forget until too late that the business of life is not business, but LIVING. — B.C. FORBES

CONTENTS

Spring 8

Summer 38

Fall 66

Winter 90

Spring

There's a hint of warmth in the air, the trees are budding and there's a red-breasted robin singing in the back yard...spring has arrived at last! It's time to pack away the heavy quilts and open the windows to enjoy the fresh air while you prepare for warmer weather. Why not greet visitors to your home with a lovely profusion of spring color? Dress the porch in sunny tulips, pretty pink petunias, crimson phlox and other blossoms; finish with a lush floral wreath on the door.

Spring has Sprung!

Celebrate Easter and the arrival of spring with Sunday brunch…and don't forget the decorations! Trim a twig tree with dyed eggs and colorful buttons, or plant grass in a painted pot and "hide" eggs for visitors to discover. For pretty little gifts, make candy eggs and embellish them with icing. Egg tree how-to's are on page 122.

HAM, BROCCOLI & CHEESE QUICHE

For my 20th birthday, my Mama, Lorry Bates, gave me an heirloom cookbook. She had various relatives and close friends write out their favorite recipes. I am sure this will be one of my treasured possessions as the years pass. It includes this recipe, which Mom has made for years.

1 c. half-and-half
5 eggs, beaten
1/2 t. dry mustard
1/4 t. pepper
1 c. cooked cubed ham
1 1/2 c. shredded Cheddar cheese
1 c. broccoli, blanched and
    chopped
1 onion, finely chopped
9-inch pie crust

To make quiche filling, combine half-and-half, eggs, mustard and pepper; set aside. Layer ham, cheese, broccoli and onion in prepared pie crust. Pour egg mixture over layers and bake for 45 to 50 minutes at 350 degrees. When a knife inserted comes out clean, remove from oven and let cool 5 minutes before slicing.

*Alicia L. Bates
Kent, OH*

PAINTED EASTER POT

Spring has sprung and Easter's on its way! How about growing your own Easter grass in a springtime flowerpot? Paint a large pot (this one is $6^3/4$" tall) with primer, then pale yellow. Use a 1" wide flat brush to paint pastel pink stripes around the pot. Trace the flower pattern from page 137 onto tracing paper, then use transfer paper to transfer flowers randomly onto the pot. Referring to *Painting Techniques*, page 134, paint the flowers purple and green with a pale yellow center, then add the green dots to the pink stripes.

To grow the grass, spread rye grass or wheat seed in a shallow dish that fits down in the pot. Lightly mist the seed with water, then place in a resealable plastic bag in a warm spot (this will create a terrarium). Now watch the seeds sprout. When the grass is the desired length, place the dish in the pot on a cake stand or can.

CANDY EGGS

There's nothing like a big candy egg for Easter, and they're oh-so simple to make! Follow the manufacturer's instructions to melt $8^1/2$ oz. of white melting chocolate…add $1/2$ oz. to 2 oz. of colored candy wafers until you have the color you want. Pour the melted candy into a clean egg-shaped soap mold that has been sprayed with non-stick vegetable spray. Allow the candy to harden and remove the egg from the mold. Use royal icing and a decorating bag with a small round tip to decorate the eggs as desired. To make the royal icing, mix 3 tablespoons meringue powder, 4 cups powdered sugar and 6 tablespoons warm water together in a medium bowl. Beat with an electric mixer for 7 to 10 minutes until stiff…this will make 3 cups of icing.

11

spring rides no horses down the hill, but comes on foot, a goose-girl still.

— EDNA ST. VINCENT MILLAY

MILK BOTTLE VASES

You can make enough of these quick & easy vases to give as party favors for your garden club meeting. Start by painting each bottle with faux etching paint. After the paint is dry, apply springtime stickers around the bottle. Tie a ribbon bow around the neck of the bottle, then fill with fresh-cut flowers from your own garden.

MILK CARRIER CENTERPIECE

Place glass milk bottles in a wire carrier. Using a continuous length of wired ribbon, tie one end of the ribbon into a bow around one bottle. Crinkling the ribbon between bottles, tie the ribbon into a bow around the next bottle. Continue until you have tied a bow around each bottle. Glue the free end of the ribbon behind the loop of the bow on the first bottle to finish the centerpiece.

BASKET OF BLOOMS

Choose a wire basket made to hang on a door. Line the basket with Spanish moss, then fill it with potting soil. Following the planting instructions for your climate, fill the basket with your favorite spring bulbs. Now, keep it watered…before you know it, you'll have springtime color that will brighten your home!

13

EMBROIDERED PIN

Trace the background pattern, page 138, onto tracing paper, then the basket onto paper-backed fusible web. Using the pattern, cut three backgrounds from muslin; cut five 1" diameter flower circles from assorted fabrics. Fuse the basket to brown fabric and cut out. Center and fuse the basket appliqué onto one background; layer the basket piece onto another background. Referring to *Embroidery Stitches*, page 133, and the stitching key on page 138, work the embroidery design through both layers of fabric. For each flower, work *Running Stitches* along the edge of one fabric circle. Pull the threads to gather, then flatten the circle to form a yo-yo. Tack the flowers to the embroidered piece. Matching right sides and leaving an opening for turning, sew the embroidered piece and remaining background together. Clip the curves, turn the pin right-side out and sew the opening closed. Beginning at the top of the pin and leaving a long ribbon streamer, work angled *Running Stitches* to attach ribbon along the edge of the pin. Tie the ribbon ends into a double bow at the top of the pin and tack to secure. Glue a pin clasp to the back of the pin.

RaBBitS have symbolized birth for many centuries and as such, represent the new life that Easter celebrates.

You'll have gifts for all ages with this cuddly chenille bunny and embroidered pin! See page 122 for the bunny instructions.

SPRING SALAD

Pick the dill for this salad early in the morning, just after the dew has evaporated.

2 c. spiral pasta
1/2 c. sliced black olives
1/2 c. red onion, chopped
10 cherry tomatoes, sliced in half
3 carrots, sliced diagonally
1 zucchini, thinly sliced
1/2 c. green pepper, chopped
1/2 c. mayonnaise-style salad
　　dressing
1/4 c. sour cream
1/2 t. garlic powder
2 t. fresh dill weed, chopped
salt and pepper to taste

Prepare spiral pasta according to directions on package. Drain, rinse and allow to cool. Combine vegetables with pasta. In a small bowl, combine salad dressing, sour cream, garlic powder and dill weed, mixing well. Blend into pasta and vegetables, coating thoroughly. Cover and chill salad one hour before serving.

Studded with sweet golden raisins and prettily decorated with colored eggs, braided Italian Easter Bread is sure to become a family favorite.

ITALIAN EASTER BREAD

Our family loves this bread served warm with butter.

1/2 c. warm water
2 pkgs. active dry yeast
1/2 c. shortening
1/2 c. milk, scalded
1/2 c. sugar
1 t. salt
2 eggs, beaten
2 t. lemon extract
4 to 5 c. all-purpose flour
1/2 c. golden raisins
Optional: 1 doz. uncooked eggs, dyed

Pour water into a large mixing bowl; add yeast and stir until dissolved. Add shortening to milk and stir until melted; cool to lukewarm.

Add to yeast mixture. Add sugar, salt, eggs and lemon extract. Blend in flour and knead until dough is smooth and elastic, about 10 minutes; knead in raisins. Shape dough into a ball and place in an oiled bowl. Cover with a towel and let rest in a warm place about 2 hours or until double in size. Divide dough into 3 portions. Roll out into equal lengths and braid. Form braid into a circle and place on a greased baking sheet. If desired, place dyed eggs between each braid or "nest" (the eggs will cook while baking). Cover and let rise 40 minutes. Bake at 350 degrees for 25 to 35 minutes.

Barb Bargdill
Gooseberry Patch

Simple pleasures are Life's Treasures. enjoy the first day of spring.

There are so many ways to turn a simple birdhouse into something fun! Search flea markets for old cabinet hardware and other vintage finds. You can even top your birdhouse with wallpaper scraps; we used solid-color embossed paper, but a colorful pattern would look charming, too. Turn to page 122 for some clever ideas...we've made it easy for you!

"I meant to do my work today — But a brown bird sang in the apple tree, And a butterfly flitted across the field."

— Richard LeGallienne

Follow instructions on the back of a package of **BOTTLE GOURD SEEDS**. Bottle gourds grow very well on a trellis, and enjoy lots of water & sunlight. Cure your gourds by placing them on a wooden rack where air can circulate around them freely. Be sure to turn them occasionally. Gourds are dry when they turn brown, beige or cream & seeds rattle loosely inside. (It may take 3 to 6 months!)

To make a birdhouse from your gourd:

1. Wash gourd in soapy water to remove dirt & mold. Let dry.

2. Using a sharp knife or fine-toothed craft saw, cut a hole in the gourd's side 1" to 1½" in diameter. The size of the hole will determine which birds will "rent" your house.

3. Remove seeds & any remaining pulp. clean inside with soapy water.

4. Spruce up the house with a painted finial, a wooden ring around the door or a wooden perch.

5. Attach a hanger and enjoy!

Herbal Harvest

Nothing adds flavor to your favorite dishes like freshly harvested herbs. Even if you're not a gardener, you can easily grow small pots of fragrant herbs on the kitchen windowsill, then snip what you need as you cook!

FLOWERPOT PLANT POKES

Use your old broken flowerpots for these fast & fun plant pokes. For each plant poke tag, *Dry Brush, page 134,* a pot piece with a "cottage" color of acrylic paint...you can paint the pots you'll be planting in at the same time. Use a permanent marker to label the tag with the name of your plant. For a stem, using pliers and starting at one end of a length of heavy-duty copper wire, twist wire around the tag to hold it in place, make a loop in the wire and trim to desired height for the pot.

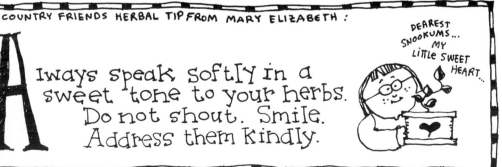

A COUNTRY FRIENDS HERBAL TIP FROM MARY ELIZABETH :

Always speak softly in a sweet tone to your herbs. Do not shout. Smile. Address them kindly.

DEAREST SNOOKUMS... MY LITTLE SWEET HEART...

Good choices for a culinary herb garden include basil, chives, dill, garlic, oregano, marjoram, mint, parsley, rosemary, sage, tarragon and thyme.

HERBED PIZZA BREAD

This delicious fresh-from-the-garden, herb-flavored pizza bread goes great with salads. It's so quick and easy...the herb spread can be made up ahead of time and kept in the refrigerator for days.

³/₄ c. unsalted butter, softened
¹/₄ c. olive oil
3 T. bread crumbs
1 T. fresh parsley, chopped
1 T. fresh chives, chopped
1 T. fresh basil or tarragon, chopped
1 or 2 cloves garlic, finely minced
salt and pepper to taste
12-inch, ready-made pizza crust
Optional: Parmesan cheese

Combine butter, olive oil, bread crumbs, parsley, chives, basil, garlic, salt and pepper until well blended. Preheat oven to 375 degrees. Spread 3 to 4 tablespoons herb butter mixture over pizza crust. Bake for 8 to 10 minutes or until golden brown. Sprinkle with fresh Parmesan cheese, if desired. Makes 1 cup spread.

Edwina Gadsby

RAW VEGETABLES WITH ARTICHOKE DIP

Surround this dip with an array of fresh vegetables...carrots, radishes, celery and peppers.

¹/₂ c. low-fat mayonnaise
¹/₂ c. non-fat sour cream
¹/₂ c. artichoke hearts, chopped
¹/₃ c. roasted red pepper
1 clove garlic, minced
2 T. fresh basil, chopped
    (or 1 t. dried basil)
¹/₈ t. dried oregano
¹/₈ t. salt
raw vegetables

Blend all ingredients together. Cover and chill one hour to allow flavors to blend. Makes 1¹/₂ cups.

Herbed Pizza Bread

Down the Garden Path

The garden can be a comforting hideaway, especially when you add accents like a rustic bench or brightly colored pots. You can even spruce up the potting shed with a handy organizer! Help a friend start her own garden with bulbs or plantings tucked in painted pots. Instructions for the bench, tool rack and large painted pots are on page 123.

Interesting planters: fill baskets, crocks, sugar buckets and galvanized tubs with flowers and herbs. If you want a really old-fashioned touch in your garden, add a weathered barrel to catch rainwater...it's so handy for watering your plants!

Add whimsy to your garden shed...the sprinkling head from a watering can makes a fun doorknob, and an old trowel can become a clever door knocker!

Cultivate the garden for the nose, and the eyes will take care of them-selves.
-ROBERT LOUIS STEVENSON

FRIENDSHIP FLOWERS

Share some of your favorite flowers with your special friends. Prime a clay pot and saucer, then paint them a springtime color. Decorate the pot and saucer with painted-on motifs of the season (we used butterflies, swirls, dot flowers and sprinkles of dots). Check out the *Painting Techniques* on page 134 for some tips from your Country Friends®. You can fill the pot different ways. In our yellow pot, we tucked a bulb and a cellophane bag of potting soil into the flowerpot, placed the saucer on the pot as a lid and tied it closed

with ribbon. Follow *Making a Tag or Label*, page 132, to add a handmade tag. For the green pot, we placed a bag of soil, tied closed with ribbon, in the pot. Now, this is easier than it looks, freeform a butterfly-shaped plant poke using $1/8$ dia. soft, pliable wire...make sure you form a loop that will hold your seed packet. Photocopy the packet pattern, page 138, onto card stock; cut out. Color the label if desired. Fold on dashed lines to assemble packet; glue flaps. Fill the packet with seeds, then attach it to the plant poke; "plant" the poke in the pot.

For memories Mom will treasure long after she's enjoyed her breakfast in bed, display the kids' artwork on a handmade tray. A tiny pin-on vase keeps a little flower bouquet fresh all day long, and the children can help craft a pretty card trimmed with pressed flowers and buttons (instructions on page 123).

MOTHER'S DAY LAP TRAY

Turn an everyday picture frame into a Mother's Day memento keeper. Prime and paint a 16"x20" wooden frame (set the glass aside), four 9" wooden legs and 4 corner leg mounting brackets white; lightly sand the wooden pieces. Using the backing from the frame as a pattern, cut pieces of hardboard and fabric to fit in the frame; apply spray adhesive to the back of the fabric and smooth onto the board. Arrange and glue keepsakes from the kids on the board. Secure the glass and the board in the frame…you may want to use screws or finishing nails to add some extra support. Attach the legs, then take the tray to Mom with her Mother's Day breakfast.

mother knows best!

BACON & CHEESE WAFFLES

For something different at breakfast, try these delicious waffles.

1 egg, beaten
1 c. milk
1 c. sour cream
1 T. butter, melted
2 c. biscuit baking mix
6 to 8 slices bacon, crisply
　　cooked and crumbled
1 c. shredded Cheddar cheese

In a medium bowl, blend together egg, milk, sour cream and butter. Stir in biscuit baking mix; blend well. Mix in bacon and cheese. Pour in enough batter to fill a preheated waffle iron and cook until steaming stops and waffles are crisp and golden. Makes 12 waffles.

Jennifer Ash
Piffard, NY

What sweeter bouquet could a mother receive than a bunch of dandelions clutched in the hands of a child?

— Nancy
Campbell

BAKED APPLE PANCAKE

So easy to prepare. While it's baking, the table can be set, sausage cooked and coffee made...perfect!

$1/4$ c. butter
4 to 5 apples, peeled, cored
　　and thinly sliced
$1/2$ c. sugar
$1/2$ t. cinnamon
6 eggs, beaten
1 c. all-purpose flour
1 c. milk
$1/2$ t. salt
Optional: maple syrup

In an $10^{1}/_{2}$" cast-iron skillet, melt butter. Add apples, sugar and cinnamon; sauté until apples begin to soften. In a mixing bowl, blend together eggs, flour, milk and salt; pour over apples in iron skillet. Bake, in iron skillet, at 375 degrees for 30 minutes or until puffed and pancake tests done in the center. Serve with maple syrup, if desired. Makes 6 servings.

Debbie Beauchamp
Murrells Inlet, SC

Perfect Planters

April showers might bring May flowers, but these country planters let you enjoy their beauty anywhere you like! You don't have to start with a new container…try painting an old metal washtub or trough, or attach holders to a worn wooden gate.

INDOOR/OUTDOOR GARDENS
Refer to Painting Techniques, page 134, before beginning your garden project.

Planter Centerpiece
Prime a metal planter, then paint it pale yellow; *Dry Brush* with soft green paint. Using the same green, paint a band around the planter, then a wavy vine over the band. Paint leaves randomly along the vine and highlight with pale yellow accents. Spray on a clear sealer to protect the surface.

Blooming Garden Gate
An old wooden gate makes the perfect backdrop for spring flowers. Lightly *Sponge Paint* a wrought-iron plant holder, a decorative wire door basket and the hinges and handle of the gate with a mossy color of green paint. Using vintage drawer pulls as the hangers, attach the plant holder and basket to the gate. Line the basket with moss, then fill the basket and plant holder with flowers.

Washtub of Flowers

Mask the top and bottom edges to make a 7" wide band around a metal planter. Paint the band cream, then *Dry Brush* with brown. Mask 1" wide borders on the top and bottom of the band; paint borders brown and remove tape. Trace the patterns, page 139, onto tracing paper. Using the patterns, cut the petal, flower center and leaf from compressed craft sponge. *Sponge Paint* flowers and leaves along the band.

Use a cotton swab to paint yellow dots on flower centers. Transfer the words along the borders…white or yellow transfer paper will show up the best. Use a liner paintbrush and cream paint or a cream-colored paint pen to draw over the transferred words.

No time for gardening? Create a Friendship Garden! Find a place for a flower or veggie patch, and with a bunch of friends, plan, prepare and enjoy the fun of gardening. Everyone should be willing to work a little every few days to keep the garden weeded and watered; plus, you should get together once a week just to chat over a glass of icy lemonade. Share the harvest…and the fun!

Decorate your hearth for spring with a flowering garden! Instructions for the "picket fence" fireplace screen are on page 123.

26

DON'T JUDGE EACH DAY BY THE HARVEST YOU REAP BUT BY THE SEEDS YOU PLANT. ~ROBERT LOUIS STEVENSON

PAINTED WINDOWBOX

To brighten an indoor windowsill, prime, then paint a wooden windowbox a creamy yellow with soft green stripes...a 1" wide paintbrush will do the trick! Use a pencil to lightly draw little flowerpots with heart flowers on the cream stripes. Paint the hearts red. Thin the red paint with a little water, then paint the pots. Use a fine-point black marker to outline the pots and flowers and to add stems for the flowers (don't forget to add detail lines to the pots). Finish your box with sprinkles of blue paint dots and fill it with potted flowers.

Friendship warms the Heart

GROUP HUG

Just as flowers brighten our gardens, friendships brighten our lives. When a good friend is under the weather (or even if she just has "spring fever"), a caring gift can bring sunshine to her day! Some thoughtful ideas…chicken soup, citrusy tea in a painted teapot, a new novel and a handmade bookmark. *To make the bookmark, turn to page 123.*

Liberal doses of garlic and onion add flavor (as well as healing properties) to Comforting Chicken Noodle Soup. To help relieve a stuffy nose, toss in a pinch of cayenne pepper.

Fun little friendship gifts: a framed snapshot of the two of you, a bottle of scented lotion, the latest book by her favorite author, coupons for free babysitting, housecleaning or lawncare.

COMFORTING CHICKEN NOODLE SOUP

Feeling under the weather? Grandma was right…chicken soup helps ease a cold.

3¹/₂ to 4 lb. chicken, halved
2 stalks celery, halved
1 onion, quartered
2 cloves garlic, minced
1 t. salt
¹/₄ t. dried tarragon
4 c. water
3 c. chicken broth
1 onion, chopped
2 stalks celery, sliced
salt and pepper to taste
¹/₄ t. dried parsley
4 oz. egg noodles, uncooked

Combine chicken and next the 7 ingredients in a large soup pot and bring to a boil. Reduce heat and simmer 45 minutes or until chicken easily pulls away from the bone. With a colander, strain the broth into a large container and discard vegetables. Remove skin and bones from chicken, chop chicken meat and set aside. Skim fat from broth and return broth to the pot. Add remaining uncooked vegetables, salt, pepper and parsley to broth. Bring to a boil, reduce heat and simmer 15 minutes. Add noodles and bring to a boil. Cook 8 to 10 minutes or according to package directions. Add cooked chicken and simmer the soup another 5 minutes.

SOOTHING TEA SET

Turn a plain white teacup & pot ensemble and a matching spoon rest into a heartfelt, thinking-of-you gift for a friend with a case of spring sniffles!

Only use Pebeo Porcelaine 150® paints to paint items and follow the manufacturer's instructions to cure the paint.

Paint the cup amber...gently rub paint to give it some texture. Paint the teapot lid and the flat area and sides of the spoon rest yellow. While the paint is drying, refer to

Stenciling, page 134, and use the lemon pattern on page 139 to make a stencil. Use the stencil to paint yellow lemon wedges around the cup.

Use your fingertip to stamp green "leaves" around the teapot and down the handle, on the lid and on the spoon rest. Use black paint and a liner paintbrush to outline the wedges and leaves, draw dotted-line stems and tendrils and to write a message around the top of the pot.

CITRUS MINT TEA
This tea is also delicious served over ice.

3 regular-size tea bags
4 to 6 sprigs fresh mint
4 c. boiling water
$^2/_3$ c. sugar
$^2/_3$ c. grapefruit juice
$^1/_2$ c. lemon juice, freshly squeezed
Garnish: lemon slices

Place tea bags and mint in a 2-quart heatproof container. Add the boiling water; cover and steep for 5 minutes. Discard tea bags and mint. Add sugar; stir to dissolve. Stir in grapefruit juice and lemon juice. Serve warm garnished with lemon slices. Makes 1$^1/_2$ quarts.

Sheri Berger

The only thing to do is to hug one's friend tight and do one's job.
~EDITH WHARTON

COUNTRY FRIENDS™ EMERGENCY KIT

PAINT AN OLD SUITCASE OR TOOLBOX TO HOLD "EMERGENCY" SUPPLIES:

chamomile Tea

Tissues

Fuzzy Slippers

Chocolate Candy

Teddy for hugging

GOOD FOR 1 ERRAND

Coupons for casseroles, errands & chores

DELIVER YOUR KIT TO A FRIEND WHO NEEDS SUPPORT OR A HELPING HAND ~ that's what friends are for!

Instructions for our "emergency" kit begin on page 123…what a great pick-me-up for a friend who's not feeling her best!

FRIENDSHIP JARS

Celebrate spring with all of your friends, co-workers, secret pals or neighbors...just hand them one of these sweet little treat jars and watch the smiles! To decorate the lid, remove the wires from an 11" length of 1¹/₂" wide wired ribbon; work *Running Stitches*, page 133, along one long edge, then glue the opposite edge around the edge of a standard-size canning lid. Pull the stitches to gather the ribbon tightly over the lid; tie the threads together and trim the ends. Use paint pens to draw lines or details on the ring part of the lid. For the handle, center an 18" length of the same ribbon over the top of a 4-oz. treat-filled jar, then twist the ring onto the jar. Knot ribbon ends together and trim with pinking shears.

Treat yourself to a good friend.

TEACUP CANDLES

What to do, what to do with all of those only-one-left, too-pretty-to-throw-away cups and saucers? Turn them into "tea-lious" candleholders for yourself or for your friends! All you have to do is purchase waxed wicks and creamy wax in your favorite springtime scent and color, then follow the manufacturer's instructions to add the wick and wax to the teacup. Simple, beautiful and quick!

Forget about the chores and go to the park with a friend. Take along a bag of popcorn and share it with the birds. The vacuuming will wait!

...all's dear that comes from a friend.

~ HORACE

BANANA ORANGE BREAD
Really a treat to give and eat!

2 c. all-purpose flour
1 t. baking powder
1 t. baking soda
1 t. pumpkin pie spice
6-oz. can frozen orange juice
    concentrate
2 ripe bananas
2 eggs
1 c. raisins
1 c. walnuts

Mix dry ingredients together. Blend orange juice, bananas and eggs; add to dry ingredients. Stir in raisins and walnuts. Pour mixture into a 9"x5" greased loaf pan and bake at 350 degrees for 35 minutes. Cool on a rack before cutting into 9 one-inch slices. May be served hot or cold, plain or with cream cheese and butter.

Ruth Palmer
Glendale, UT

Welcome to Our Neighborhood

Welcome new neighbors with a batch of cut-out cookies. Cut a card stock tag, sew on a quilt snippet and buttons, then add your message. Be sure to include your name and phone number! Watch garage sales and flea markets for vintage linens to line the basket.

some of our **best friends** live right next door...

THANK your lucky stars for a great **NEIGHBOR**.

Show your appreciation for an extra-special friend with a simple cross-stitched bouquet...and don't forget to share your handmade calling cards! See page 124 for the instructions.

HOME SWEET HOME COOKIES

What neighbor wouldn't like these heartwarming cookies?

Cookies:
1 c. butter or margarine, softened
²/₃ cup vegetable shortening
2 cups sugar
¹/₄ cup honey
2 eggs
2 t. vanilla extract
6 c. all-purpose flour
¹/₂ t. salt

Preheat oven to 350 degrees. In a large bowl, cream butter, shortening and sugar until fluffy. Add honey, eggs and vanilla; beat until smooth. In another large bowl, combine flour and salt. Add dry ingredients to creamed mixture; stir until a soft dough forms. On a lightly floured surface, use a floured rolling pin to roll out dough to ¹/₄-inch thickness. Use a 4¹/₂"x3³/₄" house-shaped cookie cutter to cut out cookies. Use a 2" heart-shaped cookie cutter to cut out cookies. Transfer to a greased baking sheet. Bake house cookies 7 to 9 minutes and heart cookies 3 to 5 minutes or until bottoms are golden. Cool on baking sheet 2 minutes. Transfer cookies to a wire rack to cool.

Glaze:
3 c. powdered sugar, sifted
4 to 6 T. milk
Red food coloring

Combine powdered sugar and milk in a small bowl; tint red. Place wire rack with heart-shaped cookies over wax paper. Spoon glaze over heart-shaped cookies. Use a small amount of glaze to "glue" to house cookies. Makes about 2 dozen.

33

Flea Market Finds

In spring, the Country Friends® can't think of anything that's more fun than making a run for the flea market! Now's the time to plan your "spring cleaning" projects…transform worn or outdated items into brand-new treasures like candlesticks, clever containers, even shelves! How-to's continue on page 124.

GLASS GLOBE CANDLEHOLDERS

Craft these beautiful yet functional candleholders with common flea market finds…wooden candleholders and glass light globes. Allowing paint and wax to dry after each application, apply primer, then brown acrylic paint to the candleholders; randomly apply paste floor wax, then paint them white. Lightly sand the candleholders over the waxed areas for an aged look. Place one globe on each candleholder. Trim taper candles shorter than the globes and place them in the candleholders.

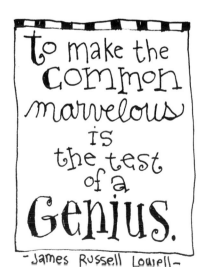

to make the
COMMON
marvelous
is
the test
of a
Genius.

-James Russell Lowell-

Everyone
L♥VeS
a
bargain.

you are my sunshine!

KNOBBY COAT RACK

Antique glass doorknobs that used to open doors can make an oh-so charming coat rack.

For each knob, drill a hole in the center of an unfinished decorative wooden accent piece. (Drill bit should be the same size as a bolt that will fit each knob.) Wipe accents with a tack cloth, then lightly *Dry Brush, page 134,* each accent brown.

Arrange accents on an unfinished wooden plaque and mark the mounting hole placement; drill holes, then wipe plaque with a tack cloth. Apply a thick coat of red pre-colored crackle medium to the plaque and let it dry. Apply a layer of green acrylic paint over the crackle medium and let it dry.

Thread bolts, from back to front, through the holes in the plaque. Thread one accent onto each bolt, then twist one knob onto the bolt.

Attach heavy-duty sawtooth hangers to the back of the rack.

GO SHOPPING with a FRIEND.

While you're at the flea market this weekend, keep an eye out for a little red wagon to paint for the Fourth of July (turn to page 43 for a sneak peek)!

Things may come to those who wait, but only the things left by those who hustle. — Abraham Lincoln

Dye a battered basket a pretty color...just mix a packet of dye in an old washtub, following packet directions. Wearing rubber gloves, dip basket into the dye, constantly moving it. Remove from dye bath and let it dry on several layers of newspaper over a sheet of plastic. When dry, add decorative hand-painted ants, stars or flowers on each strip...a wonderful picnic basket idea!

You won't believe how simple it is to create this handy message center using an old frame and wooden shutters! The complete instructions are on page 124.

*S*ummer

Oh, the long, lazy days of summer, with its sunny skies and outdoor adventures! Take time to enjoy the beauty of nature...go for walks (or bicycle rides!) early in the morning, nurture your garden in the afternoon and spend the evenings relaxing on the porch. You can create a welcoming mini-garden at your front door with pots of colorful zinnias, periwinkle and yellow kalanchoe; wind mandevilla vines 'round the columns and plant plenty of four-o'-clocks and other flowering plants along the walkway.

Handmade Father's Day gifts are a terrific way to say, "Dad, you're the best!" Decorate a lapboard with the kids' artwork, make a handyman's snack caddy or fill a big, personalized bowl with munchies...try our zesty mix of popcorn & peanuts. Instructions for the bowls are on page 124.

Of all nature's gifts to the human race, what is sweeter to a man than his children? ~ CICERO (106-43 BC)

Hey, Mom! Now's the time to "clean up" the refrigerator door...use the kids' drawings to decorate a lapboard for Dad.

DAD'S LAPBOARD

Dad will love showing off the kids' artwork on a lapboard he can use while watching television this Father's Day!

Paint a wooden lapboard the desired color, then paint stripes along the edges...remember to let the paint, sealer and glue dry after each application. Spray the fronts and backs of your selected artwork with clear acrylic sealer, then use decoupage glue to adhere them to the board...you may want to glue black photo mount corners to a few of the treasures, or have the kids use paint pens to write endearing words on the board. Paint polka-dots randomly on the board, then apply 2 to 3 coats of sealer to the entire board.

CARRY-ALL JAR TOTE

Give Dad a treat and a handy portable storage tote, too!

Use screws to attach the lids from 3 jars to the bottom of a wooden plaque…be sure the screws do not go all the way through the plaque. Use decoupage glue to adhere paper cut-outs to the top of the plaque, then apply 2 to 3 coats of clear acrylic sealer. Use screws to attach a door handle to the top center of the plaque. Fill the jars with treats or goodies Dad will enjoy and twist the jars onto the lids. Refer to *Making a Tag or Label*, page 132, to make a tag to go with the tote.

DAD'S POPCORN & PEANUTS

A quick snack for Dad and the gang!

$1/3$ c. butter, melted
1 t. dried dill weed
1 t. Worcestershire sauce
$1/2$ t. garlic powder
$1/2$ t. onion powder
$1/4$ t. salt
2 qts. popped popcorn
2 $1^1/2$-oz. cans potato sticks
1 c. mixed nuts

In a large mixing bowl, blend first 6 ingredients together well. Add popcorn, potato sticks and nuts. Toss mixture and place on an ungreased baking sheet. Bake at 350 degrees for 3 minutes; stir mixture and bake another 4 to 5 minutes. Makes 9 cups.

Shelley Turner
Boise, ID

41

Red, White & Blue S·A·L·U·T·E

Give an all-American salute to summer with an old-fashioned picnic! You'll need plenty of red, white & blue decorations…how about a super-simple porch swag, or an easy-to-paint mailbox cover? Or you can fix up that little red wagon to use as a patriotic planter. The porch swag instructions begin on page 124.

PATRIOTIC MAILBOX COVER

Your home will shine with American pride when you decorate your mailbox with this easy-to-do wooden cover.

Start by cutting 14 wooden lattice strips the same length as your mailbox. Spacing ¼" apart, arrange the strips wrong-side up on a flat surface; leaving about 10" at each end of the wire free, staple 16-gauge wire 3" from each end to hold the strips together. Apply wood-tone spray to the strips, then randomly apply paste floor wax (when sanded, this will create an aged look). Paint half of the middle 6 strips blue; alternating colors, paint the strips red or white. *Sponge Paint*, page 134, white stars on the blue strips. Randomly sand the strips, wipe with a tack cloth and apply 2 to 3 coats of clear acrylic sealer. Arrange the cover on the mailbox; twist the wire ends together under the mailbox to secure.

To create a whimsical planter-on-wheels, use white acrylic paint to dry-brush stripes on a red wagon, then use a liner brush to add blue stars and write patriotic sayings around the rim…like "God Bless America," "Land That I Love," "United We Stand," "Freedom For All" and "My Home Sweet Home." Read our Painting Techniques on page 134 before you start.

PICNIC BARBECUED CHICKEN SANDWICHES

These are delicious hot or cold, depending on where you'll be enjoying them.

3 lbs. chicken thighs and breasts, skinned, cooked, boned and shredded
1 c. catsup
1³/₄ c. water
1 onion, finely chopped
1 t. salt
1 t. celery seed
1 t. chili powder
¹/₄ c. brown sugar, packed
1 t. hot pepper sauce
¹/₄ c. Worcestershire sauce
¹/₄ c. red wine vinegar
6 Kaiser rolls

Combine all ingredients except rolls in large saucepan and simmer for 1¹/₂ hours. Pile onto rolls. Serve warm or chill meat and make into sandwiches. Pack in a thermal container with ice and serve cold.

Summertime is cookout time, and there are plenty of patriotic occasions to celebrate while school's out. Invite your family, the neighbors and all the kids for a day of fun in the sun and serve traditional barbecue, potato salad and deviled eggs (Celebration Deviled Eggs recipe is on page 46). You can show your independence with a rick-rack flag pin (great for favors, too), a star-spangled tablecloth and painted flowerpots. The craft instructions are on page 125.

GARDEN-FRESH NEW POTATO SALAD

Watch it disappear!

1½ lbs. new potatoes, cubed
¾ lb. fresh green beans, snapped
1 sweet red pepper, chopped
1 red onion, chopped
½ c. vegetable oil
¼ c. cider vinegar
2 T. Dijon mustard
1 t. fresh parsley, chopped
1 t. fresh dill weed, chopped
1 t. sugar

Cook potatoes in boiling water 10 minutes, add green beans and bring to a boil. Continue boiling until potatoes are tender. Drain and allow to cool. In a large serving bowl, add sweet red pepper and onion to cooked potatoes and beans. Combine remaining ingredients and pour over vegetables. Toss to coat; chill thoroughly before serving. Serves 12.

FRESH TOMATO SALAD

This dish is at home with a more elegant meal or your basic backyard gathering!

4 yellow tomatoes, chopped
4 red tomatoes, chopped
2 cucumbers, peeled and chopped
1 red onion, thinly sliced
3 to 4 sprigs fresh basil, chopped
salt and pepper to taste
1 c. vinaigrette dressing
Garnish: fresh basil

Combine all ingredients in a clear glass bowl; toss. Serve immediately at room temperature. Garnish with basil. Makes 6 to 8 servings.
Carla Meredith
Belchertown, MA

Use colorful cotton bandannas instead of paper napkins at your picnic. Tie one around each set of utensils. After the party, just toss them in the washer.

Summertime favorites...Fresh Tomato Salad, Picnic Barbecued Chicken Sandwiches, Garden-Fresh Potato Salad and Home Run Bean Bake (recipe on page 46).

QUICK SUMMER SLAW

A GUARANTEED PARTY PLEASER... EVERYONE WILL WANT THE RECIPE!

PACKAGE OF COLE SLAW MIX
1 BUNCH GREEN ONIONS, CHOPPED
½ c. SHELLED SUNFLOWER SEEDS
½ c. ALMONDS, SLIVERED & SLICED
½ c. OIL
3 T. SUGAR
3 T. CIDER VINEGAR
PACKAGE CHICKEN-FLAVORED NOODLES

TOSS SLAW MIX, GREEN ONIONS, SUNFLOWER SEEDS & ALMONDS TOGETHER IN A BOWL. IN A SMALL BOWL, WHISK TOGETHER OIL, SUGAR, VINEGAR & SEASONING PACKET FROM NOODLES 'TIL WELL BLENDED. POUR OVER SLAW AND MIX. CHILL. JUST BEFORE SERVING, STIR IN DRY, CRUSHED NOODLES.

★VARIATIONS~ TRY BALSAMIC, HERBAL OR RASPBERRY VINEGAR IN PLACE OF CIDER VINEGAR. SUBSTITUTE HOT & SPICY CHICKEN-FLAVORED NOODLES FOR A ZINGY FLAVOR.

CALIFORNIA LEMONADE

Cardamom is a fragrant spice from India that tastes much like cinnamon.

1½ c. sugar
1 c. lemon juice, freshly squeezed
5 cardamom seeds, ground

Combine sugar and lemon juice in a small saucepan. Boil at medium heat for 8 to 10 minutes. Add cardamom seeds and store in refrigerator. To prepare lemonade, mix one tablespoon of concentrate with one cup sparkling water.

CELEBRATION DEVILED EGGS

Between me, my 4 brothers and sisters and our children, there are 10 birthdays and 3 anniversaries in the summer months! Along with graduations, Father's Day and the 4th of July, we do a lot of celebrating…any excuse to get together!

12 eggs, hard-boiled
½ c. mayonnaise
2 T. onion, chopped
1 t. fresh chives, chopped
1 t. fresh parsley, chopped
1 t. dry mustard
½ t. paprika
½ t. dried dill weed
¼ t. salt
¼ t. pepper
¼ t. garlic powder
milk
Garnish: paprika and parsley

Remove shells from eggs. Cut eggs in half lengthwise and remove yolks. Place yolks in a shallow bowl and mash with a fork. Add rest of ingredients, except milk, to egg yolks. Stir. If necessary, stir in a little milk to achieve the desired consistency. Spoon the yolk mixture into the egg-white halves. Cover and chill before serving. Makes 24.

Barb Bargdill
Gooseberry Patch

HOME RUN BEAN BAKE

Baked beans are always a favorite side dish at our home. Great served with bratwursts or hamburgers…always a hit!

1 lb. dry red kidney beans
1 lb. dry great Northern beans
1 T. salt
1 lb. Kielbasa, sliced
2 T. water
3 onions, chopped
2 10-oz. bags frozen lima beans, thawed
2 baking apples, cored, peeled and chopped
4 cloves garlic, chopped
¾ c. molasses
¾ c. tomato sauce
½ c. Dijon mustard

Rinse and sort beans. Place beans and salt in a large saucepan, cover with water and bring to a boil. Boil 2 minutes, turn off heat and cover pan; let sit one hour. In a heavy skillet, cook Kielbasa and water over medium heat 10 minutes. Add onions and continue to cook until Kielbasa is browned, about 10 minutes. Remove from skillet and set aside. Drain soaked beans, reserving cooking liquid. Place beans in a 6-quart casserole dish, add lima beans, apples and garlic. Stir in Kielbasa mixture. Combine molasses, tomato sauce and mustard; stir well. Pour evenly over bean mixture. Add just enough reserved bean cooking liquid to cover the beans. Cover casserole dish and bake at 350 degrees for 1½ hours. Reduce heat to 275 degrees and continue to bake for another 6 hours. Add more liquid to beans to keep them moist during baking. Serves 16 to 20.

Helen Murray
Piketon, OH

Be sure to save room for dessert! For rave reviews, try treats like Deluxe Ice Cream Sandwiches, refreshing Fruit Compote or My-Oh-My Peach Pie.

My Oh My Peach Pie

We dECLARE! THE BEST PEACH PIE I EVER DID EAT!

4 c. PEACHES, QUARTERED & PEELED
1/2 c. SUGAR
1/2 t. NUTMEG
DASH SALT
1 EGG
2 T. CREAM

1/2 c. ALL-PURPOSE FLOUR
1/4 c. BROWN SUGAR, PACKED
2 T. BUTTER
9" UNBAKED PIE SHELL

ARRANGE PEACHES IN PIE SHELL ~ SPRINKLE WITH SUGAR, NUTMEG & SALT. BEAT EGG & CREAM ~ POUR OVER PEACHES. MIX FLOUR, BROWN SUGAR & BUTTER 'TIL CRUMBLY, THEN SPRINKLE OVER PIE. BAKE AT 425° FOR 35 TO 45 MINUTES.

FRUIT COMPOTE

Perfect for summer's delicious bounty of berries, peaches, nectarines, melons and cherries…refreshing endings for any picnic!

Syrup:
1 c. water
1/2 c. sugar
3/4 c. fresh mint, chopped
1 T. fresh lemon juice
Optional: 1/4 c. bourbon

Compote:
1/4 cantaloupe, seeded
1/4 honeydew, seeded
1/2 lb. sweet cherries, pitted
3 ripe peaches, thinly sliced
3 T. fresh mint, thinly sliced
Garnish: fresh mint sprigs

To make syrup, combine water and sugar in a medium saucepan over low heat until sugar dissolves. Add mint and boil 5 minutes over medium heat. Let cool completely. Strain mixture into a bowl, pressing firmly on the mint to extract flavor. Mix the lemon juice and bourbon into the syrup. Cover and refrigerate; can be made ahead of time. For compote, scoop melons with a melon baller. Combine all fruits; add syrup and toss. Refrigerate for 30 minutes. Spoon into pretty pedestal glasses or into a watermelon half and garnish with mint sprigs.

DELUXE ICE CREAM SANDWICHES

We like these chewy, thin oatmeal cookies

Cookies:
1 c. butter, melted
4 c. long-cooking oats, uncooked
1 c. all-purpose flour
1 t. salt
1 1/2 c. sugar
1/2 c. brown sugar, packed
2 t. vanilla extract
2 eggs, lightly beaten

Sandwiches:
1/2 gallon natural vanilla ice cream
Garnish: sprinkles

Combine butter, oats, flour, salt, sugars and vanilla: stir well to combine. Add eggs and mix thoroughly. On a baking sheet that has been covered with parchment paper, spoon 1 1/2 tablespoons of batter for each cookie, leaving about 3 inches between cookies. Flatten cookies into 3" circles. Bake until golden, about 10 minutes. Let cool. Makes 2 dozen. Unwrap block of vanilla ice cream and slice into 1-inch thick slices, cutting into squares big enough to slightly overlap edges of cookies. Sandwich ice cream between cookies. Dip edges of sandwiches into sprinkles. Wrap individually and freeze until ready to serve.

Make pretty raspberry ice cubes for your lemonade! Halfway fill each compartment of an ice-cube tray with water; freeze. Place a fresh, whole raspberry on each ice cube, fill compartments with water and freeze until solid.

Hey BATTER • BATTER • BATTER
PLAY BALL!

Enjoy some old-fashioned fun with your neighborhood friends! Set up an area outside for a game of horseshoes, softball, tug-of-war, scavenger hunt or Red Rover. It's a terrific way to play together.

Put together kid-safe party packs for the youngsters to enjoy! Decorate a white pail with stickers (you may need to use spray adhesive and finish with clear acrylic sealer if you're using a metal bucket), then fill with goodies…noisemakers, plastic bubble wrap for popping, mini flags, flashlights with fiber-optic sprays, silly sunglasses, etc.

Host the "Summer Olympics" for neighborhood kids. Keep the events fun…have kids balance feathers on their heads while carrying water balloons, run races holding inflated beach balls between their knees and target-shoot with the garden hose! Make fun "medals" for all!

✶ROLL BEACH BALLS WITH YOUR NOSE ⌣ RACE ACROSS THE LAWN! ✶ PICK UP PENNIES WITH YOUR TOES OFF THE BOTTOM OF THE SWIMMING POOL ★ WASH YOUR BIKES IN THE HOSE ⌣ GET GOOD & WET ! ✶

Backyard ★ FUN ★ Waterpark

✶ RUN THROUGH THE SPRINKLERS ★ WATER·BALLOON TOSS ★ GET PRUNY-TOED IN THE POOL! ✶ EAT DRIPPY ORANGE POPSICLES AND RINSE OFF IN THE GARDEN HOSE ★ MAKE MUD PIES & WET SAND CASTLES

Gather 'round a bonfire! Just make a quick phone call to invite the neighbors, and before you know it, you'll have your backyard filled with eager kids and parents! Everyone will love an evening spent together under the stars playing flashlight tag, hide-and-seek, storytelling and toasting marshmallows. If you live in an area where you can't have open fires, use the barbecue grill instead!

Simple Garden pleasures

Capture the simple beauty of an old-fashioned summer garden with a bouquet of fresh ideas…a trio of stitched flowers, "sew-simple" pillows, a dried rose wreath and a charming topiary in a pastel-striped pot. To make the pillows and framed florals, turn to page 125.

Create your own romantic summer hideaway, right on your very own porch. Decorate with white wicker, white tablecloths, crocks full of flowers, candles and white trellises on the sides of the porch. Create as much shade as possible. Add some old flowery cushions and some iced tea or lemonade, and sit there as much as possible with those you love!

— Deb Damari-Tull

SUMMER WREATH

Simple & elegant is what this wreath is. We used dried flowers and naturals on our wreath, but if you grow a garden chock-full of summer offerings, feel free to use them instead.

Begin with a wreath made from dried naturals. Arrange and glue shelf fungi (spray the fungi with sealer before adding it to the wreath), dried flowers and grass along the bottom of the wreath. Fill in any holes with more dried flowers. Tie one yard of ribbon into a bow with several loops and glue it to the wreath. Thread craft wire through the top back of the wreath and twist the ends together for a hanger. Now! you're ready to display this natural beauty for all to enjoy.

SUMMER TOPIARY

The delightful scents of summer are beautifully displayed in this handpainted clay pot...oh-so simple to make, and you can enjoy them for a long time!

Prime, then paint a 6" diameter clay pot light yellow; paint darker yellow vertical stripes around the pot under the rim. Lightly sand the pot, then wipe with a tack cloth and apply a coat of clear acrylic sealer.

Fill the pot with plastic foam. Use a craft knife to cut a hole at the center of the foam. Gather a layer of dried white daisies around a bunch of larkspur, then a layer of dried lavender around the daisies; secure stems with a rubber band. Place the stems in the pot, then glue dried sheet moss over the foam. Tie a length of ribbon into a bow around the stems, covering the rubber band.

Use pretty ribbons to bundle stems of Sweet Annie and hang them on your fence posts or gate. Every time you brush against them, they'll release a sweet fragrance.

CHeerY CHerrieS

Who could resist the colorful appeal of orchard-fresh cherries?
Give your kitchen a sweet summertime makeover…add accessories
like a painted teakettle and stitch up pretty towels, an apron and
a whimsical pot holder! Instructions continue on page 125.

Make "instant" kitchen curtains from print cotton dish towels! Place a tension rod across the lower half of the window and use clip-on café curtain rings to hang towels lengthwise. To make a matching valance, simply hang towels horizontally from a second tension rod.

Cheery Cherry Tea

a recipe from Michelle Campen
* Peoria, IL

15-oz. jar orange drink mix
1 c. sugar
1 c. unsweetened instant tea
½ c. lemonade powder
0.13-oz. pkg. cherry drink mix
2 t. cinnamon
1 t. nutmeg

Blend all ingredients together well and store in an airtight container. Makes about 5 cups of dry mix.

CHERRY TEAKETTLE

No patterns needed...using acrylic paint for metal, you can turn a plain old white teakettle into a cheery kitchen accessory.

Using a flat brush in the desired width for your squares, paint a checkerboard border along the bottom of the teakettle. Paint plump red cherries with green stems around the kettle...add green leaves to the stems. Paint a small highlight of white on each cherry, accent the leaves and stems with yellow and add a black highlight at the base of each stem. Use the end of the paintbrush to add dots randomly around the teakettle and let the paint dry.

HAND TOWEL

Transform a purchased kitchen towel with checkerboard stripes into one that looks like you spent hours on it. Sew jumbo rick-rack along the inner edge of one border, then work embroidery floss *Backstitches*, page 133, along the opposite edge and the edges of the next stripe.

For the cherries, cover three 1⅛" diameter buttons from a covered button kit with red fabric. Sew the cherries to the towel, then work embroidery floss *Backstitches* for the stems. Fold a length of green grosgrain ribbon into 3 loops, then sew the center of the loops at the top of the stems.

CHEERY CHERRY
TEA
Stir 1 to 2 tablespoons of tea mix in 1 cup of hot or cold water.

Add cheer to the breakfast table with a table topper and matching chair pads…trim them with jumbo rick-rack and oversize buttons just for fun! Instructions for the chair cushions and covers are on page 126.

CHERRY TABLE TOPPER

Our topper fits a 20" square table…if your table is a different size, cut your square to fit and cut your border pieces the same length as one side of the square.

Cut a 28" square of fabric; cut four 28" long pieces from border fabric. Turn the short and bottom edges of the border pieces 1/4" to the wrong side and sew in place. Matching right sides and raw

edges, center, then sew one border piece to each side of the square…sew jumbo rick-rack over the seam lines and a button at each corner of the topper.

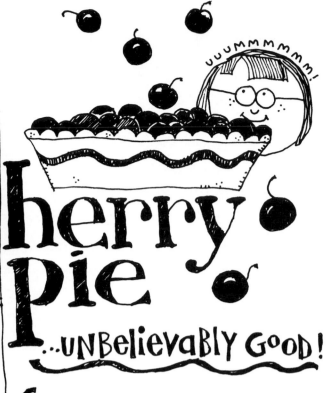

Cherry pie

...UNBELIEVABLY GOOD!

INGREDIENTS:

- 🍒 PASTRY FOR A DOUBLE-CRUST PIE OR TWO ALREADY-PREPARED PIE CRUSTS
- 🍒 1 - 1½ C. SUGAR
- 🍒 4 T. MINUTE TAPIOCA
- 🍒 4 C. PITTED TART RED CHERRIES — FRESH, FROZEN OR CANNED
- 🍒 ½ t. ALMOND EXTRACT OR ½ t. CINNAMON
- 🍒 1 T. MARGARINE
- 🍒 OPTIONAL: RED FOOD COLORING

Combine sugar & tapioca in saucepan. Fold in fresh or frozen cherries; blend well. (If using canned cherries, drain juice from fruit and mix juice with sugar & tapioca in saucepan. Set aside cherries.)

Cook over medium heat, stirring constantly,'til mixture has come to a boil. Remove from heat.

Add extract & butter. (Add canned cherries at this time.) One drop of food coloring may be added to enhance color. Cool mixture before placing in pie crust shell.

While filling is cooling, prepare pie crust according to recipe if making from scratch.

Line bottom of 9" pie pan with one rolled pie crust dough. Place cooled filling in pie shell. Cut slits in second pie crust and place on top of cherry filling. Seal & flute edges.

Bake at 400° for 30 - 35 minutes.

When selecting fresh cherries, choose the ones that are firm, plump and blemish-free with bright, glossy skin. Store fresh cherries in the refrigerator for no more than three days (use a plastic bag with holes to allow air circulation). Remove stems and wash just before eating...what a sweet treat!

PIE BIRD FAN PULL

Oh-so clever...a fan pull to catch the eye!

Choose a colorful ceramic pie bird, then cut 20" lengths of chenille yarn, rick-rack and ½" wide fabric strips in colors that coordinate with the bird.

For the tassel, bundle the strips together and wrap a length of craft wire several times around the middle, leaving the wire ends long. Fold the bundle in half and secure the wire ends tightly around the end of a pull chain; trim the wire ends. Thread the opposite end of the chain up through the pie bird, pulling the tassel up into the bird.

The summer harvest provides a fresh medley of flavors that make it easy to add a little home-grown zip to your menus. If you're not a gardener, visit the farmers' market for a wonderful selection of fruits & veggies. Here are some of our favorite garden treats…enjoy the tastes of summer!

Clockwise from lower left: Hot Peach Jam, Fresh Corn-Tomato Salsa, Confetti Salad with Herbal Dressing, Bread & Butter Pickles, Tomato-Pepper Relish, Summer Tomatoes

CONFETTI SALAD

You may use bottled dressing, or make our Herbal Dressing.

1 zucchini, shredded
1 carrot, shredded
1 green pepper, shredded
1 yellow squash, shredded
1 sweet red pepper, shredded
$1/3$ c. vinaigrette or sweet and sour
    dressing

Combine vegetables and toss with dressing. Serves 4 to 6.

HERBAL DRESSING

Try this tasty dressing on Confetti Salad or a mix of fresh greens from the garden.

$1/2$ t. pepper
$1/2$ t. fresh chives, finely chopped
$1/2$ t. fresh parsley, finely chopped
$1/2$ t. fresh tarragon, finely
    chopped
1 clove garlic, finely minced
10 T. olive oil
3 T. wine vinegar
1 t. Dijon mustard
$1/2$ t. salt

Place all ingredients together. Blend with wire whisk.

> Marlene Wetzel-Dellagatta

Some herbs can help your vegetables grow! Plant basil, borage, chives and parsley near tomatoes to enhance flavor and repel pests. Mint drives away white cabbage moths, but keep it contained or it'll take over your garden! Dill helps your cabbage grow, but keep it away from carrots and tomatoes. Thyme stimulates overall growth in the garden.

"To get the best results, you must talk to your vegetables."

> *— Charles, Prince of Wales*

EASY PICKLED PEPPERS

A mix of hot and mild peppers that's great in salads or on sandwiches.

1 qt. vinegar
3 c. water
2 c. oil
$2/3$ c. salt
$1/4$ c. dried oregano
$1/4$ c. celery seed
4 cloves garlic, minced
8 qts. mixed hot and sweet
    banana peppers, sliced into
    rings
1 stalk celery, sliced

Combine vinegar, water, oil, salt, oregano, celery seed and garlic in a heavy saucepan; bring to a boil. Place peppers and celery in a large heatproof bowl; pour boiling mixture over peppers and celery until just covered. Cover and let stand at room temperature for 8 hours, stirring occasionally. Put into jars and keep refrigerated. Makes 8 quarts.

> Kristie Rigo
> Friedens, PA

SUMMER TOMATOES

There is nothing better in the summer than tomatoes…home grown with loving care on a patio or in a backyard garden.

4 tomatoes, sliced
1 red onion, sliced into rings
1 green pepper, sliced into rings

Alternate layers of above vegetables in a big, wide bowl.

Marinade:
$1/4$ c. lemon juice
2 T. fresh parsley, chopped
$1/2$ t. sugar
1 t. salt
$1/2$ c. oil
$1/8$ t. dried savory
$1 1/4$ oz. blue or Roquefort cheese

Mix lemon juice, parsley, sugar, salt, oil and savory. Pour over layered veggies. Sprinkle crumbled cheese over top. Marinate overnight in refrigerator to blend flavors. Serve as a side dish.

> Ruth Kangas

Summer Tomatoes

ZESTY ONION RELISH

Use the grill to make this relish and grill the main course...a wonderful condiment for chicken, pork or beef.

2 lbs. onions, thickly sliced
1/4 c. canola oil
3 T. balsamic vinegar
2 T. brown sugar
1/4 t. cayenne pepper

Lightly brush onion slices on each side with oil. Place onions on grill and cook over low heat for 15 minutes or until tender and golden. Turn onions to brown each side, coating again with oil as needed. Remove onions from grill and allow to cool. Chop onions and set aside. Simmer vinegar and brown sugar in a saucepan over low heat. Stir until sugar has dissolved then pour over onions. Sprinkle cayenne pepper over top and stir again. Serve warm, refrigerating any leftovers.

GARLIC DILL PICKLES

For a really different pickle, try substituting fresh rosemary or tarragon for the dill.

13 1/2 c. white vinegar
13 1/2 c. water
2 1/4 c. pickling salt
1 1/2 c. pickling spices
10 lbs. cucumbers, 2" to 3" long,
    thoroughly cleaned
12 cloves garlic, peeled and minced
15 stems of fresh dill

Combine the vinegar, water, salt and spices to make a brine and bring to a boil in a large pot. Fill hot, sterilized quart jars with the cucumbers, garlic and dill; cover with the hot brine. Leave 1/2" headspace at top of each jar. Wipe the rims and adjust the lids. Process in a boiling water canner for 15 minutes.

FRESH CORN-TOMATO SALSA

A delicious, spicy chip dip...or spoon on top of Spanish rice.

1 c. fresh corn, cooked
1 ripe tomato, peeled, seeded
    and chopped
1 cucumber, peeled, seeded
    and chopped
1 onion, finely chopped
1 celery stalk, chopped
1 jalapeño pepper, chopped
3 T. lime juice, freshly squeezed
1/2 t. cumin
1 garlic clove, minced
1/2 t. salt

In medium bowl, stir together all ingredients until mixed well. Cover and refrigerate, allowing flavors to blend for at least an hour.

TOMATO-PEPPER RELISH

This makes a delicious Christmas relish to share during the holidays.

1 gallon green tomatoes, chopped
8 red peppers, chopped
2 onions, chopped
2 c. white vinegar
2 c. sugar
2 T. salt
1 T. celery seed
2 sticks cinnamon
2 T. whole allspice
2 T. whole cloves

Combine green tomatoes, peppers, onions, vinegar, sugar, salt and celery seed. Stir in cinnamon, allspice and cloves or add to mixture in a spice bag. Bring vegetables to a boil. Reduce heat and simmer for 15 minutes. Ladle into hot, sterilized pint jars, leaving 1/2" headspace. Wipe rims and adjust lids. Process in a boiling water canner for 15 minutes. Makes 10 pints.

HOT PEACH JAM

Delicious on crackers with cream cheese, as an ice cream topping or a glaze for ham!

1 1/2 c. cider vinegar
1/4 c. jalapeño pepper, quartered,
    or other green chili pepper
5 c. fresh peaches, finely chopped
6 c. sugar
1 t. celery seed
1 t. allspice
2 3-oz. pouches liquid pectin

Combine vinegar and pepper in blender. Process to desired fineness. Combine with peaches, sugar, celery seed and allspice in large pot (not aluminum) and bring to a boil. Reduce heat and simmer 50 minutes, stirring often. Let cool 2 minutes, then add pectin. Ladle into hot, sterilized pint jars, leaving 1/4" headspace. Wipe rims and adjust lids. Process in a boiling water canner for 5 minutes. Makes 10 cups.

Sonia Bracamonte
Tucson, AZ

Get an early start on Christmas gifts...set aside some of your best home-canned goodies to share!

RADISH JELLY

Serve with cream cheese and crackers or spread on a roast beef sandwich.

2 c. radishes, finely chopped
2½ c. sugar
¾ c. water
1¾-oz. pkg. pectin
2 t. prepared horseradish

In a large saucepan, combine radishes, sugar and water over medium-high heat, stirring constantly until sugar dissolves. Bring to a rolling boil. Add pectin; stir until dissolved. Bring to a rolling boil again and boil 1 minute longer. Remove from heat and skim off foam. Stir in horseradish. Ladle into sterilized jars and seal; cool. Store in refrigerator. Makes about 2 pints.

Marie Alana Gardner
North Tonowanda, NY

Zippy Vegetable Casserole

MAKE IT AHEAD OF TIME & STORE IN THE FRIDGE UP TO 24 HOURS... YUM!

3 c. Fresh Plum tomatoes, seeded & chopped
3 c. zucchini, chopped
3 medium onions, chopped
3 cloves garlic, minced
¼ c. fresh parsley, minced
¼ c. fresh basil, finely chopped
1 c. mozzarella cheese, shredded
2½ c. bread crumbs

Coat two 7"x11" baking dishes with nonstick vegetable spray. Place tomatoes, zucchini, onions, garlic, parsley & basil in baking dishes. Mix together cheese & bread crumbs. Toss 1½ c. of the crumb mixture with veggies. Sprinkle remaining crumbs over top of veggies. Refrigerate until ready to bake. Bake at 350° for about 45 minutes.

The time to *Relax* is when you don't have time for it.

~ Sydney J. Harris ~

ZUCCHINI RELISH

Zucchini is always a favorite from my garden. This relish is great served on steak sandwiches, hamburgers or hot dogs. It's also a perfect hostess, teacher or Christmas gift!

10 c. zucchini squash, chopped
4 c. onions
4 T. salt
2½ c. vinegar
3 c. sugar
1 t. turmeric
½ t. pepper
¼ t. dry mustard
½ t. mustard seed
3 peppers (2 green and 1 red)

Grind squash and onions; add salt. Refrigerate overnight. Drain. Run clear water through the ingredients several times. Drain again. Put ingredients in a large kettle. Add vinegar, sugar, turmeric, pepper, dry mustard and mustard seed. Grind green and red peppers. Add to squash mixture. Stir gently. Bring to a boil and cook 3 minutes. Ladle into 8 hot, sterilized pint jars, leaving ½" of headspace. Wipe rims and adjust lids. Process in a boiling water canner for 10 minutes. Makes 8 pints.

Janet Myers
Reading, PA

Be sure to follow the USDA-recommended water-bath method when canning. Your local Cooperative Extension Service will have the most up-to-date information on canning, and may even offer canning workshops!

When canning, always select fresh, healthy, ripe fruits and vegetables; wash well.

Use real sugar only...don't use artificial sweeteners, sugar substitutes or sugar blends when canning. Never double jam or jelly recipes, as the mixtures may not set properly.

61

Making Memories

Make the most of a summer afternoon…gather your friends for a scrapbooking party! Ready-to-use pressed flower stickers make it easy to give the invitations a cottage garden look. Ask your guests to bring along their family photos and creative supplies, then spend the afternoon sharing ideas and memories.

CANDIED VIOLETS

These delicate edible confections can be used as decorations on cakes or simply put out for nibblers on a glass plate. Both scent and flavor are exotic. You can also candy fresh mint leaves and other edible flowers. We used violas to match our party invitations.

16-oz. pkg. pasteurized egg whites
perfect, pesticide-free violets and
    leaves
sugar

Whip egg whites until they're frothy but do not stand in peaks. Wash violets and leaves gently and quickly in cold water and let water drip off. While damp, dip each violet or leaf in the egg white and roll it quickly in sugar to coat evenly, taking care not to get the sugar too thick. Lay on wax paper, without overlapping, to dry. After several hours or a day, the blossoms will be quite crisp and can keep for several months without losing fragrance or flavor. Store in airtight container, layered between wax paper. Makes dozens.

Juanita Williams
Jacksonville, OR

FLOWER INVITATION

Announce your memory-making day with this beautiful invitation.

Tear a piece of handmade paper into a rectangle to fit on the front of a blank card; use a craft glue stick to adhere the paper to the card. Overlapping and gluing ends at front, wrap a length of ribbon around the front of the card. Use decorative-edge craft scissors to cut a tag from card stock. Write a message on the tag, then glue the tag to the card. Arrange and adhere self-adhesive botanical stickers to the card. Simple to make!

PRETTY LITTLE CAKES

These pretty little cakes make every party a special one.

Cake:
18¼-oz. pkg. white cake mix
1⅓ c. water
2 T. vegetable oil
3 egg whites
2 t. almond extract

Icing:
10 c. sifted powdered sugar
1 c. water
3 T. light corn syrup
1 t. vanilla or almond extract
Garnish: candied violets

Preheat oven to 350 degrees. For cake, line bottom of a greased 15½"x10½" jelly roll pan with wax paper; grease wax paper. In a large bowl, combine cake mix, water, oil, egg whites and almond extract. Prepare according to package directions. Pour batter into prepared pan. Bake 18 to 22 minutes or until a toothpick inserted in center of cake comes out clean and top is golden. Cool in pan 10 minutes. Invert cake onto a wire rack and cool completely. Transfer cake to baking sheet covered with wax paper. Freeze cake 2 hours or until firm. Using a serrated knife, cut away sides of cake to straighten. Cut cake into 2-inch squares. Place squares 2 inches apart on wire racks with wax paper underneath.

For icing, combine powdered sugar and remaining ingredients in a large saucepan; cook over low heat, stirring constantly, until smooth. Quickly pour warm icing over cake squares, completely covering top and sides. Spoon all excess icing into saucepan; reheat until smooth. (If necessary, add a small amount of water to maintain icing's original consistency.) Continue pouring and reheating icing until all cakes have been iced twice. Garnish each cake with candied violets. Let icing harden completely. Trim any excess icing from bottom edges of each cake square. Store cakes in an airtight container. Makes about 40 cakes.

Delightful indulgences…Pretty Little Cakes garnished with Candied Violets, accompanied by Refreshing Mint Punch.

REFRESHING MINT PUNCH

I love this! It's such a nice change from traditional punch.

2 c. mint leaves, packed
2 c. water
12-oz. can frozen lemonade
1 qt. ginger ale

Bring mint and water to boil; bruise leaves with potato masher. Set aside overnight. Strain and discard solids. Add lemonade, 3 lemonade cans of water and ginger ale to mint mixture; mix well and serve. Makes 10 to 12 servings.

Mary Murray
Gooseberry Patch

A smiling face is half the meal.
- LATVIAN PROVERB -

FLORAL SCRAPBOOK

Turn a plain and simple photo album into a sweet memory album. Use decorative-edge craft scissors to cut a piece of handmade paper the size you want for the front of your album; glue it in place. Use a permanent marker to write your family name on a shipping tag; tie a piece of ribbon through the hole in the tag, then glue the tag to the paper. Overlapping as desired, adhere self-adhesive botanical stickers around the edges of the paper and tag.

MEMORY PAGES

Using acid-free papers and adhesives, arrange your photographs on the album pages. To preserve your photos, do like we did and use photo-mount corners to hold them in place. Use small shipping tags to identify the photographs...add ribbons and floral self-adhesive botanical stickers to the pages as desired. Make the pages extra-special by attaching pieces of lace or doilies that belonged to the cherished people in the photos.

Of all nature's gifts to the human race, what is sweeter to a man than his children? ~ CICERO (106-43 BC)

Make a scrapbook of family photos to preserve the joys of ordinary days! You'll love recalling a day in the life of your family. Snap candid photos of sleepyheads in their beds at 6 a.m, the 7 a.m. toothbrush brigade, schoolwork, chores...all through the day! Make notes in your book beside each photo in your own handwriting...a lasting memory of a regular, wonderful day!

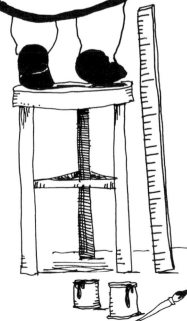

WHAT AN IDEA !

A DAY IN THE LIFE OF YOUR FAMILY

Fall

Autumn arrives in a vibrant blaze of color, with bright blue skies and brilliant foliage in shades of red and gold. It's time to unpack your cozy sweaters and light a fire in the hearth...time to send the children off to school and get set to cheer for the local football team! To celebrate the bountiful harvest, adorn your entryway with pots of colorful chrysanthemums and basketfuls of pumpkins, squash and fragrant apples. Swirl bittersweet along the porch railing and treat the front door to a handsome arrangement of dried flowers and grasses.

SCHOOL DAYS

Who could forget the excitement of the first day of school? Riding the school bus, a fresh box of crayons, a shiny lunchbox and making new friends. It's all those little things that stir up the fondest memories.

Remember your lunchbox from grade-school? Give it a fresh look with autumn motifs and pack it full of naturally delicious Chewy Granola Bars! See page 127 for the instructions.

CHEWY GRANOLA BARS

These are great for snacks or dessert served warm with ice cream. I sometimes substitute 1/2 cup of cocoa for half of the flour for an extra chocolate delight!

1/2 c. margarine, softened
1 c. brown sugar, packed
1/4 c. sugar
2 T. honey
1/2 t. vanilla extract
1 egg
1 c. all-purpose flour
1 T. cinnamon
1/2 t. baking powder
1/4 t. salt
1 c. quick-cooking oats, uncooked
1 1/4 c. puffed rice cereal
1 c. chopped pecans
1 c. raisins
1 c. chocolate chips

Cream margarine, sugars, honey, vanilla and egg, mixing well. Combine all dry ingredients and add to creamed mixture. Press into a greased 13"x9"x2" baking pan and bake at 350 degrees for 22 to 28 minutes. Let cool; cut into bars. You can substitute peanut butter chips or butterscotch chips for the chocolate if you like. Makes 16 bars.

Laura Flournoy
Columbus, NC

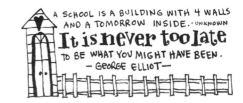

A SCHOOL IS A BUILDING WITH 4 WALLS AND A TOMORROW INSIDE. -UNKNOWN
It is never too late TO BE WHAT YOU MIGHT HAVE BEEN. — GEORGE ELLIOT—

PAINTED NAMEPLATE

The only rules here are to let the primer, paint and sealer dry after each application and to use hot glue for all gluing.

Apply primer, then white paint to a wooden plaque. Paint checkerboards, a few stars and stems for cherries on the plaque. Use a fine-point marker to outline the stars and draw dots around them. Use a black paint pen to write your name really big on the sign, then apply 2 to 3 coats of sealer. Sharpen a wooden pencil and glue it to the plaque. Glue 2 big red buttons on the sign for cherries and a knotted strip of homespun at the top of the stems for leaves.

Show your appreciation for a special teacher with a personalized nameplate for the classroom or a colorfully decorated denim vest; the vest instructions are on page 127.

END ZONE BROWNIES

So easy...add chocolate chips for even more rich flavor.

1/2 c. butter
1 c. sugar
4 eggs
16-oz. can chocolate syrup
1 c. plus 1 T. all-purpose flour
1 t. vanilla extract
1 c. chopped walnuts
Garnish: powdered sugar

Mix all ingredients together and pour into a 15"x10" greased jelly roll pan. Bake at 350 degrees for 20 to 22 minutes. Cool 10 minutes; remove from pan and dust with powdered sugar. Makes 2 1/2 dozen.

★ GOALS ★

are dreams with deadlines.

-Diana Scharf Hunt-

PACK·A·SACK

PERFECT PACKAGING FOR PICNICS, TAILGATE LUNCHES OR KIDS' PARTIES!

STEP ONE: PUT EVERYTHING YOUR GUEST WILL NEED INSIDE A LUNCH-SIZE BAG... (CHOOSE SCHOOL-COLORS FOR TAILGATE LUNCHES, OR TEAM HUES) SANDWICH, COOKIES, WHATEVER!

STEP TWO: FOLD OVER TOP OF BAG AND PUNCH 2 HOLES NEAR TOP.

STEP THREE: SLIDE PENNANT STICK, PENCIL OR STRAW THROUGH HOLES TO KEEP BAG SHUT.

STEP FOUR: GIVE ONE BAG LUNCH TO EACH GUEST AND EAT UP!

During autumn, the high school grandstand is always full for the Friday night football game, so cheer on your team! Pack a basket of goodies to enjoy while the marching band performs at halftime…crunchy apples, spicy molasses cookies and a thermos filled with warm cider would be just right.

Support your local football team at the big game! Stitch up a cozy blanket and hot water bottle cover in school colors and carry along a basketful of chocolatey End Zone Brownies for munching. To make the blanket and bottle cover, see page 127.

A HAUNTING We Will Go

Make your house "eerie-sistible" to little ghosts and goblins this Halloween. Our crew of felt-face Jack-'O-Lanterns and glowing luminaries are sure to do the trick!

FELT-FACE PUMPKINS

These faces-of-the-season are safe & easy for children to create...no knives or carving involved! Use a copy machine to size your favorite face pattern from page 146 to fit your pumpkin. Cut out the pattern...child safety scissors will work. Draw around the shapes on the paper side of self-adhesive felt, then cut out the shapes. Peel the paper from the cut-outs and adhere the face to your pumpkin. For Jill-'O-Lanterns, tie a strip of Halloween-motif fabric into a big bow around the stem, and you're done. These are quick enough to do even on a school night!

SIDEWALK LUMINARY

For each luminary, fill a plastic zipping bag with water and put into a small tin pail and freeze overnight…this will keep the pail from bending when you punch the holes.

Draw a face on your pail. Use a hammer and awl to punch holes inside the drawn lines and one hole on each side of the pail for the handle. Remove the bag of ice.

Allowing the paint to dry after each application, place the pail upside-down and apply orange stained glass spray paint to the outside.

Paint the face shapes with black.

Trace the leaf pattern from page 147 onto tracing paper and cut out. Use the pattern to cut one leaf from craft tin; punch a hole in the leaf. Paint the leaf green.

For the handle, thread the ends of a length of green craft wire through the holes on each side of the pail; place the leaf on one end of handle, then curl and twist the wire ends to secure. Place a candle in the pail, then hang the luminary on a short garden hook.

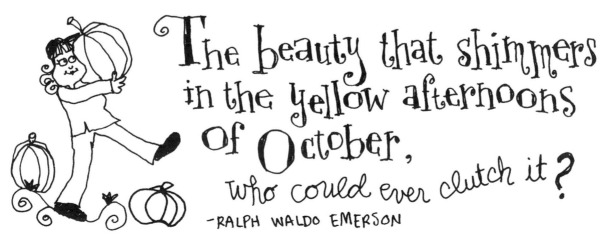

The beauty that shimmers in the yellow afternoons of October, who could ever clutch it?

—RALPH WALDO EMERSON

An autumn welcome…a basket of gourds and pumpkins by the mailbox and corn shocks tied around the post. Top bunches of Indian corn with raffia bows and drape on either side of the basket.

CREEPY CRAWLY SPIDERS

This is a super-simple creepy project for the kids to make. Use a craft stick to hold two foam balls together for the body…we used a 2¹/₂" and a 4" diameter ball. Paper maché over the spider body using craft glue and small pieces of tissue paper. After the spider is dry, paint it black. Cut 4 bumpy pipe cleaners in half for legs; stick four legs into each side of the body. Cut 2 bumps from another pipe cleaner and stick into the head for antennae. For each eye, thread one bead onto a large-head straight pin…stick eyes into spider.

OCTOBER IS GOOD FOR A SCARE!

Enjoy a Halloween bonfire…roast hot dogs and marshmallows, drink cocoa and tell ghost stories!

Jack-'O-Lantern Patch instructions on page 128.

"BOO" WELCOME MAT

A simple painted mat is a "boo-tiful" idea to welcome friends into your home. Use a copy machine to enlarge the patterns on page 149 to fit a sisal mat…ours came with the black fabric binding. Cut out the letters and arrange them on the mat. Use a marker to lightly draw around each letter; repeat for the candy corn pattern. Paint the designs. After the paint is good and dry, use a black paint pen to outline the candy corn sections. Finish off with a strip of green grosgrain ribbon glued along the inside edges of the binding.

Enjoy the tastes of autumn with a loaf of Harvest Pumpkin Bread and a jar of Roasted Pumpkin Seeds. The homespun pumpkin pins are so easy to make that you'll have a whole pumpkin patch in no time!

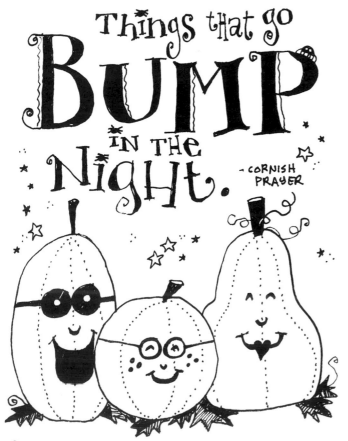

Things that go BUMP IN THE NIGHt.

~ CORNISH PRAYER

HARVEST PUMPKIN BREAD

Dress up this bread with raisins or walnuts if you like.

2 c. all-purpose flour
1 c. brown sugar, packed
1 t. cinnamon
1/4 t. nutmeg
1/8 t. ground cloves
1 T. baking powder
1/4 t. baking soda
1/4 t. salt
1 c. canned pumpkin
1/2 c. milk
1/3 c. butter or margarine, softened
2 eggs

Preheat oven to 350 degrees. Grease a 9"x5" loaf pan. Combine one cup of flour, brown sugar, cinnamon, nutmeg, cloves, baking powder, baking soda and salt in mixing bowl. Add pumpkin, milk, butter and eggs and beat on low until blended; increase speed to high and beat for 2 minutes. Gradually add remaining flour and beat until well mixed. Pour batter into loaf pan and bake for 60 to 65 minutes.

PUMPKIN PINS

For each pin, layer cotton batting between the wrong sides of two 4" squares of pumpkin-colored homespun. Trace the desired pumpkin shape from page 147 onto tracing paper and pin to the squares. Leaving an opening at the top of the pumpkin to fit a small twig for the stem, sew along the lines of the pattern, then carefully tear away the paper. Use pinking shears to cut out the shape just outside the outer sewn lines. Hot glue the stem between the fabric layers, then glue a jewelry pin back to the back of the pumpkin. For the leaves, cut a ½"x4" strip from green fabric; knot strip around the stem.

ROASTED PUMPKIN SEEDS

2 c. seeds
1 T. oil
½ t. salt
·········
Rinse pumpkin seeds — dry on paper towels. Toss with oil. Place on baking sheet and bake at 350° for 20 minutes. Toss every 5 to 7 minutes. Remove from oven when golden brown. Salt ∴ eat up!

PUMPKIN SEED JAR

This jar is oh-so quick to make and perfect to hold a batch of roasted pumpkin seeds from your carved Jack-'O-Lantern. Spray paint the outside of the lid from a wide-mouth glass jar. Tie several strands of raffia into a bow around the neck of the jar.

BLACK CATS and GOBLINS and GHOSTIES...

OH*MY!

Here's a spooky idea for a children's Halloween party game! First, select objects that are "creepy" to touch…try olives in a glass of water for eyeballs, a leaf for a bat's wing, scraps of torn cotton balls for spiderwebs, a pickle for a witch's nose and rawhide sticks for a skeleton. Place each object in a separate box, then drape with black fabric and label as "Dead-Man's Eyes," "Sleeping Bat's Wings," etc. Let one child at a time reach into the boxes and try to guess what the objects REALLY are!

TOMATO COSTUME

As easily as the Fairy Godmother changed the pumpkin into a coach, you can change your wee one into a too-cute tomato! First, you'll need two pieces of red felt...when folded in half, each piece needs to reach from elbow to elbow and hang from the shoulder to 3" below the knees on the child. Open the felt pieces, place them together and refold. At the center of the fold, use a dinner plate to mark a half-circle for the head opening; cut out the circle. Place the felt pieces over the child's head. Tie a piece of ribbon around each shoulder to gather the felt...it's okay to tie the ribbon at the top of the shoulders because it will be on the inside when you're finished. Now, mark the armholes on each side of the costume, then take it off the child. Time to sew up the sides...only sew up to the marks and sew through all four layers of felt! Sew the felt layers together around the bottom edge. For the elastic casing, fold the bottom edge up 1 1/2" and pin in place. Leaving an opening to insert the elastic, sew along the casing edge. Turn the costume right-side out and place it back on the child. Insert 3/4"w elastic in the casing and adjust to desired tightness and height around the legs. Trim the elastic and secure with a safety pin. Working through the armholes, stuff the tomato to desired plumpness...you can use fiberfill, plastic bags or foam peanuts.

(continued on page 128)

Even if you're short on time, you can "treat" your child to a unique Halloween costume. Choose from a funny bug, a plump tomato, a fancy fairy or a ferociously friendly lion. Instructions for the bug, fairy and lion costumes are on page 128.

"Everything is black and gold, black and gold, tonight: Yellow pumpkins, yellow moon, yellow candlelight: Jet-black cat with golden eyes, shadows black as ink, firelight blinking in the dark with a yellow blink. Black and gold, black and bold, nothing in between. When the world turns black and gold, then it's Halloween!"

— Nancy Byrd Turner

GIMME CANDY!

HALLOWEEN POPCORN BALLS
A fun Halloween treat for all ages.

1 c. light corn syrup
1/4 c. margarine
2 T. water
1 1/3 c. powdered sugar
1 t. salt
24 large marshmallows
1/2 t. vanilla extract
5 qts. popped corn, no salt
12-oz. pkg. candy corn pieces

In a heavy saucepan, combine corn syrup, margarine, water, powdered sugar, salt and marshmallows over medium-high heat. Stir until smooth and mixture just comes to a boil. Remove from heat; stir in vanilla. Place popcorn in a large roasting pan. Pour hot mixture over popcorn; toss to coat. Let mixture cool a few minutes before handling. Stir candy corn pieces into popcorn mixture. Wet hands with a very small amount of water and form popcorn balls. Press very firmly with hands when forming balls or they will fall apart! Place on wax paper to cool. Wrap each popcorn ball in cellophane and tie closed with a piece of raffia. Makes one dozen.

Great goodies for kids: candy corn and popcorn are a yummy combination. Place wrapped Halloween Popcorn Balls in a "witch's cauldron" by your front door. Youngsters will also love biting into Marshmallow Cookie Spiders.

MARSHMALLOW COOKIE SPIDERS
Spooky but sweet, these spiders are easy to fix for school parties.

black licorice rope for legs
4 1/4-oz. tube white icing
9-oz. pkg. chocolate-
    covered marshmallow
    cookies
assorted candies for eyes

For each spider, cut 4 pieces of licorice measuring from 2" to 3" in length. Using a knife, cut each licorice piece in half lengthwise. Place each pair of legs opposite each other, flat side down, on lightly greased wax paper. Cover inside ends of licorice with icing. Gently press cookie onto icing and legs. Use icing to "glue" the candies onto cookie for eyes. Allow icing to set up and carefully transfer cookie spiders to serving plates. Makes 8 spiders.

PAINTED TREAT POTS

Make your treats extra-special by giving in one of these handpainted clay pots. Trace the pumpkin pattern on page 149 onto tracing paper; use transfer paper to transfer several pumpkins around a 4" diameter pot (ours was already painted white). Allowing the paint to dry after each application, paint the pumpkins, then a checkerboard around the bottom of the pot. Use a black permanent marker to outline and add details to the pumpkins and draw dots and tiny stars around them. Apply 2 to 3 coats of clear acrylic sealer to the pot, give it plenty of time to dry, then fill with goodies

STAMPED TREAT BAGS

These bags are so easy...the kids can make them for school treats. Trace the leaf pattern on page 149 onto tracing paper. For each bag, use the pattern to cut one leaf from green corrugated craft cardboard; punch a hole in the leaf. Stamp pumpkins on a brown lunch-size paper bag; use colored pencils to color them. Fill the bag with treats and surprises, then gather the top of the bag; secure with a green pipe cleaner. Thread the leaf onto one end of the pipe cleaner, then curl the ends.

AUTUMN LigHts

Light up an autumn evening with glowing candles and pumpkin lanterns…they're a snap to make with these quick & easy ideas!

CANDLE JARS

It just wouldn't be fall without the enchanting glow of dancing shadows produced by flickering candlelight. For each of these candles, follow the manufacturer's instructions to melt and fill a clean glass jar with candle wax and a purchased wick. For the label, use a copy machine to size and reproduce a nostalgic seasonal clipping or postcard to fit on the jar. Cut out the label and glue it to card stock, then trim the card stock just a bit larger than the label…glue it to the jar. (You may need to use rubber bands to hold the label in place until dry.) Cut a tag from card stock; punch a hole in one end. Stamp a message on the tag, then use raffia to attach the tag to the jar.

CARVED FAUX PUMPKINS

All that work…and something to show for it year after year! Try carving faux pumpkins for creations that last. You can use pre-made carving kits and patterns, or come up with your own ideas, then carve them just like real pumpkins. Be creative! Try filling holes with flat accent marbles or painting the carved areas yellow for a fun glow. If your pumpkin didn't come with a light, simply add a clip-on light kit through the back of the pumpkin.

Pumpkins weren't grown in Europe many years ago, so children used to carve turnips for Halloween. When colonists in America planted their crops, pumpkins were more plentiful than turnips, and our modern Jack-'O-Lantern was born!

For me, autumn is a time to really make my house cozy. I like to buy several pumpkins, placing some on my front porch along with the potted plants, and also on the tabletops throughout my house. I also fill baskets with pretty fall leaves and small, colorful gourds and hang Indian corn, tied with raffia, on my front door and over the fireplace, giving a real "harvest" feel to the house. Candles in the holders and lamps change from pastels to dark, rich, autumn colors. Bowls are filled with fragrant potpourris, and place mats and runners are changed to heavier weaves.

— Nancie Gensler

All-cheering plenty,
with her flowing horn,
led yellow autumn,
wreath'd with nodding corn.
— BURNS

Dress pillar candles to coordinate with your autumn décor...turn to page 129 for creative ideas!

There is
no season
when such
PLEASANT
and sunny spots
can be lighted on,
and
produce so pleasant
an effect on the feelings,
as now in
OCTOBER.
— HAWTHORNE —

FLORAL PLACE CARD

Make any place setting special with this beautifully personalized place card. Cut a 4³/4"x5¹/2" card from corrugated craft cardboard; match short edges and fold in half. Use decorative-edge craft scissors to cut a 2¹/2"x4¹/2" piece from card stock. Cut a 2¹/4"x4¹/4" piece from decorative paper. Glue the card stock piece, then the decorative paper piece on the folded card. Stamp your guest's name on the place card. For the finishing touch, cover the name with a length of sheer ribbon; glue the ribbon ends to the inside of the place card to secure.

LEAF LIGHT-CATCHER

Quick to make, yet elegant to display...that's what this sun-catcher is! Arrange silk or preserved leaves between two 4"x6" panes of glass. Apply a strip of ¹/2" wide self-adhesive copper foil across the top edge of the panes. Cut another length of copper for the handle; trim the paper from the ends and attach to the light-catcher. Starting at the top of one side, cover the remaining edges with copper.

Use the vibrant colors of autumn…crimson, gold, copper and russet to make this beautiful wreath to greet family & friends. Gather a variety of dried flowers (bittersweet, globe amaranth, cockscomb, statice, sunflower heads and preserved leaves work really well), and then carefully hot glue them on a grapevine wreath. You can also tuck in a few silk blooms for added color. Add a loop of wire to the back of your wreath and it's ready to hang in no time!

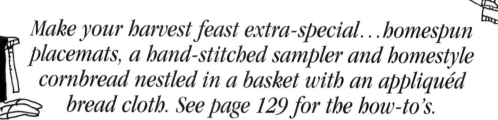

Season of Thanks

Make your harvest feast extra-special…homespun placemats, a hand-stitched sampler and homestyle cornbread nestled in a basket with an appliquéd bread cloth. See page 129 for the how-to's.

COUNTRY CORNBREAD

You can leave out the jalapeño and still have a terrific country-style cornbread, but you really should try it with the pepper. Either way, it's great served with a bowl of homemade soup.

1¼ c. cornmeal
¾ c. all-purpose flour
5 T. sugar
2 t. baking powder
½ t. salt
1 c. buttermilk
⅓ c. vegetable oil
1 egg, lightly beaten
1 c. sharp Cheddar cheese, finely shredded
1 c. whole kernel corn
1 T. fresh jalapeño, seeded and minced

In a large bowl, mix together cornmeal, flour, sugar, baking powder and salt. Make a well in the center of the mix and pour in the buttermilk, oil and egg. Stir until ingredients are lightly moistened. Fold in cheese, corn and jalapeño. Pour mixture into lightly oiled 8"x8" baking dish. Bake at 375 degrees for 25 to 30 minutes, or until a tester inserted in the center comes out clean. Let cool slightly, cut into 2-inch squares. Makes 16 servings.

Missy Collier
Buellton, CA

TURKEY-VEGETABLE CHOWDER

This is a terrific, hearty chowder made using your leftover turkey!

1/4 c. butter
2 onions, chopped
2 T. all-purpose flour
1 t. curry powder
3 c. chicken broth
1 potato, chopped
1 c. carrots, thinly sliced
1 c. celery, thinly sliced
2 T. fresh parsley, minced
1/2 t. dried sage or poultry
    seasoning
3 c. cooked turkey, chopped
1 1/2 c. half-and-half
10-oz. pkg. frozen chopped
    spinach
Garnish: parsley leaves

Melt butter in a small Dutch oven. Add onions and sauté for 10 minutes. Stir in flour and curry powder. Cook for 2 minutes. Add broth, potato, carrots, celery, parsley and sage. Reduce heat to low. Cover and simmer 10 to 15 minutes. Add turkey, half-and-half and frozen spinach. Cover and simmer, stirring occasionally until heated through, about 10 minutes. Makes 8 cups.

Robyn Fiedler
Tacoma, WA

Happy Thanksgiving!

"Hurrah for the fun!
Is the turkey done?
Hurrah for the pumpkin pie!"
— Lydia Maria Childs

 I could be READING ...

 I could be LOOKIN' ...

 But I'm GIVIN' THANKS...

 'CAUSE I AIN'T COOKIN'!

Fabric leaves serve as napkin holders on our checked placemats...add button-on nametags just for fun! See page 129.

HOLIDAY JAM

Easy-to-make jam...make some to give and some for your family to enjoy.

1 c. fresh cranberries
10-oz. pkg. frozen strawberries, thawed
2 c. sugar

Put cranberries into a blender, cover and chop by turning on and off, on and off, etc. Empty into saucepan; add strawberries and bring to a boil. Add sugar and boil until thickened. (It doesn't thicken a lot.) Pour into jelly glasses. Jam may be stored in refrigerator for 2 to 4 weeks.

Judy Norris

MULLED CIDER

Try cider instead of coffee once in a while...cut down on caffeine and enjoy the pure taste of fall!

2 qts. apple juice or sweet cider
½ c. brown sugar, packed
2-inch cinnamon stick
1 t. whole allspice
1 t. whole cloves
Garnish: long cinnamon sticks

Mix apple juice or cider and sugar in large saucepan. Add spices. Heat mixture slowly to simmering. Cover pan, simmer 20 minutes and strain. Serve hot, with a cinnamon stick in each mug.

Harvest Fruit and Nut Pie

COMBINE THE FRUITS OF THE HARVEST IN THIS DELICIOUS PIE!

4 9-inch FROZEN DEEP-DISH PIE CRUSTS

4 GRANNY SMITH APPLES, PEELED & SLICED

1 C. CRANBERRIES
½ C. PINEAPPLE TIDBITS, DRAINED
½ C. CHOPPED WALNUTS
1 C. SUGAR
2/3 C. BROWN SUGAR, PACKED
4 T. ALL-PURPOSE FLOUR
1 t. CINNAMON
¼ t. NUTMEG
3 T. BUTTER

THAW 2 PIE CRUSTS AND FLATTEN FOR TOP CRUSTS. STIR TOGETHER APPLES, CRANBERRIES, PINEAPPLE, WALNUTS & SUGAR. SIFT TOGETHER BROWN SUGAR, FLOUR, CINNAMON & NUTMEG; ADD TO APPLE MIXTURE. DIVIDE EQUALLY BETWEEN 2 PIE CRUSTS; DOT EACH WITH BUTTER AND COVER WITH TOP PIE CRUSTS. BAKE AT 400 DEGREES FOR 45 MINUTES. MAKES 2 PIES.

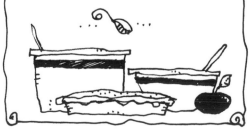

Top jars of Holiday Jam with batting and homespun and decorate with buttons...great for sharing with friends & neighbors!

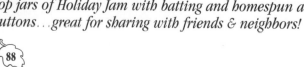

What would Thanksgiving dinner be without Spicy Pumpkin Pie topped with dollops of whipped cream? And instead of the traditional mincemeat, try the delicious mixture of apples, cranberries and walnuts in our Harvest Fruit & Nut Pie...it's heavenly!

SPICY PUMPKIN PIES

Makes 2 large pies for a family gathering or 4 small pies for sharing.

29-oz. can of solid-pack pumpkin
2 c. brown sugar, packed
3 T. pumpkin pie spice
1 t. salt
5 eggs, lightly beaten
2 12-oz. cans evaporated milk
2 10" deep-dish pie crusts or
   4 9" pie crusts, unbaked
Garnish: fresh whipped cream

In a large bowl, whisk pumpkin, brown sugar, spice and salt until well blended. Whisk in the eggs. Slowly whisk in the evaporated milk until completely blended. Pour the filling into the pie crusts. Bake at 375 degrees for 40 to 50 minutes or until the pies move very slightly in one mass when lightly jiggled. Transfer pies to a wire rack for cooling. Serve with plenty of fresh whipped cream.

Be Thee Thankful for your happy family. Tell them so.

When the brisk autumn breezes become cold and blustery, we know that winter's on its way, and with it comes the festive holiday season! The short days and long nights provide wonderful opportunities to enjoy the warmth of a crackling fire, a mug of chocolatey cocoa and the company of family & friends. You'll want to extend a cheery greeting at the door...crimson ribbons and pots filled with winter-blooming amaryllis add merry touches to the traditional evergreen and holly decorations on the front porch.

*Our motto is "the more the merrier" when it comes to collecting snowfolk!
Just like us, they come in all shapes, sizes and styles. If you're just starting
out, a set of three or four will grow into an extended snow family in no
time! We've got some friendly fellows to add to your collection, plus a
whimsical display shelf; instructions for the shelf begin on page 129.*

GOURD SNOWMAN

Use a craft stick to spread textured snow medium on a gourd. Drill arm holes and a nose hole in the gourd. Find a twig "nose" and two twig "arms" in the yard...glue them in the holes. Paint the nose orange; paint small pebbles for eyes, mouth and buttons black. Glue the pebbles in place.

For the scarf, sew buttons on a strip of fleece; work *Straight Stitches*, page 133, for snowflakes on the scarf. Cut narrow strips in the ends of the scarf for fringe.

For the hat, turn a child-size sock wrong-side out, then sew from heel-side bottom of cuff to toe to shape the hat; trim seam allowance and turn right-side out. For the tassel, cut four 1"x3" pieces from fleece, stack together and tie around the center...cut narrow strips in the ends for fringe. Sew the tassel on the hat. Fold the cuff of the hat up for a brim and sew buttons on it.

SNOWMAN PIN

Stack 2 pieces of felt together. Use pinking shears to cut a snowman shape from the felt pieces. Leaving small openings for arms and an opening for stuffing, sew shapes together close to the edge. Lightly stuff, then sew the opening closed. Cut the end from an orange toothpick for the nose. Glue the stick arms in the armholes, the nose on the face and a pin clasp to the snowman. Use a colored pencil to add the cheeks and a black permanent marker for the eyes and mouth. Knot a torn strip of homespun around the snowman for the scarf.

SNOWMAN CUPS

For each cup, paint a gourd bell cup white, then lightly *Sponge Paint*, page 134, with thinned light blue. Paint pink cheeks on the cup...add a white highlight on each cheek. Use black dimensional paint to paint a face on the cup and orange dimensional paint to sculpt a nose. Use white dimensional paint to paint a squiggly line along the top front of the cup; while paint is still wet, apply iridescent glitter.

Drill a small hole on each side of the cup at the top. For the handle, curl the ends of a length of craft wire around a pencil, then thread the ends through the holes.

Winter Warmers

When the cold winds blow, there's nothing better than coming home to a hearty meal and a cup of hot chocolate! Share the warmth with a friend…decorate fleecy mittens with snowflakes and fill with goodies.

MIKE'S GRANDMA'S CHILI

Add more chili powder to make it as hot as you like!

1 lb. ground beef
1 c. onions, chopped
1 clove garlic, minced
15-oz. can kidney beans, undrained
1 qt. tomato juice
$1/2$ t. cumin
1 t. chili powder
1 t. salt
$1/2$ t. pepper
1 t. oregano
$1/2$ c. brown sugar, packed

In a large soup pot, cook ground beef, onions and garlic until meat is browned and crumbly. Add remaining ingredients and simmer on low for 30 minutes or longer. Makes $6^{1/2}$ cups.

For a quick and tasty treat, try adding a little extra flavor to your favorite packaged cocoa...cinnamon, chocolate syrup or sweetened condensed milk. Adults will love a splash of amaretto or butterscotch schnapps, and whipped cream with sprinkles will bring out the kid in anyone!

FLEECE MITTENS

Fleece mittens for frosty fingers...add a button and embroidered snowflake and you have a quick & cozy gift! To make the snowflake, sew on several different-sizes of white buttons to form a cross shape, then add white *Running Stitches* and *French Knots*, page 133, to make a star. To trim the cuff, sew the edges of a length of ribbon over the elastic on the mitten; remember to stretch the elastic as you sew...this will ensure that the cuff will still stretch when it's put on. Fill the mittens with goodies for extra fun.

CANDY CANE HOT CHOCOLATE MIX

Yummy cocoa mix with a taste of peppermint...a cozy gift!

1½ c. powdered sugar
1 c. plus 2 T. baking cocoa
1½ c. nondairy creamer
20 peppermint candies, broken into pieces
mini marshmallows

In a one-quart wide-mouth jar, layer powdered sugar, then cocoa, packing each layer as tightly as possible. Wipe the inside of the jar with a paper towel to remove any excess cocoa before adding the next layer. Add nondairy creamer to jar, packing tightly. Add peppermint pieces. Fill any remaining space in top of jar with a layer of mini marshmallows; secure lid. Give with the following instructions: Empty jar into a large mixing bowl; blend well. Spoon mixture back into jar. To serve, add ¾ cup boiling water to ¼ cup cocoa mixture; stir to blend. Makes 16 servings.

Mary Deaile
Fresno, CA

95

SPAGHETTI PIE

A great family meal; just add a salad and some garlic bread!

1/2 lb. spaghetti, cooked
2 eggs
1/4 c. grated Parmesan cheese
1/2 t. salt
1/4 lb. sliced pepperoni, divided
2 c. mozzarella cheese, divided
2 c. spaghetti sauce

Combine spaghetti, eggs, Parmesan cheese and salt. Mix thoroughly. Grease 13"x9" baking dish and place half of mixture in bottom. Layer top with half of pepperoni and mozzarella cheese, then layer with remaining spaghetti mixture. Add remaining pepperoni and mozzarella cheese. Bake for 15 to 20 minutes at 350 degrees. Cut into squares and serve topped with sauce.

Eleanor Bierly
Miamisburg, OH

Country Friends Casserole

a recipe from Holly

2 T. butter
1 c. celery, chopped
1/4 c. onion, chopped
2 10-3/4-oz. cans cream of mushroom soup
2/3 c. chicken broth
4 c. chicken, cooked & diced
4 T. soy sauce
2 c. rice, cooked
1 c. chow mein noodles
1 c. cashews

In large saucepan, sauté celery & onion in butter 'til tender. Stir in soup & broth~ simmer 5 minutes. Add chicken & soy sauce. Cook over low heat 5 minutes. Stir in rice. Pour into 13"x9" baking dish and bake at 375 degrees for 20 minutes, or 'til liquid is bubbling. Sprinkle noodles & nuts on top. Brown in oven. Serves 8 to 10.

Yum! Top the Country Friends® Casserole with crispy noodles and serve Pistachio Whip for a light dessert.

PISTACHIO WHIP

Keep these ingredients on hand for a light and fruity dessert.

2 12-oz. cartons frozen whipped topping
2 16-oz. cans pineapple tidbits and juice
2 3.4-oz. pkgs. instant pistachio pudding mix

Combine whipped topping and juice from pineapple. Add pistachio pudding and mix well. Add pineapple and mix well.

LaVerne Biunno

Slow-Cooker Beef Stroganoff

START IT IN THE MORNING ~
ENJOY IT IN THE EVENING!

1 LB. LEAN ROUND STEAK CUBES
1 ENVELOPE DRY BEEFY ONION SOUP MIX
10 3/4-OZ. CAN CREAM OF CELERY SOUP
10 3/4-OZ. CAN CREAM OF MUSHROOM SOUP

Place all items in slow-cooker. Cook on low for 6 to 8 hours, stirring occasionally. Serve over cooked noodles or rice. (For a delicious variation, stir in 1/2 c. sour cream.)

Hearty fare: Cheesy Bread, Slow-Cooker Beef Stroganoff and Red and Green Slaw.

Freeze summer vegetables to enjoy year 'round. Create a "soup mix" by combining corn, carrots, celery, onion, broccoli, tomatoes and potatoes for hearty winter soups and stews.

RED AND GREEN SLAW

Yes, sweet red peppers are costly, but they are so good...you deserve one!

1 1/2 c. green cabbage, chopped or
   very thinly sliced
1/2 c. red cabbage, chopped or
   very thinly sliced
1/2 red pepper, very thinly sliced
   in long strips

Dressing:
1/4 c. mayonnaise
1 t. lime juice
1/4 t. sugar
1/4 t. garlic
salt

Combine cabbages and pepper. Combine dressing ingredients; stir into cabbage mixture. Serves 8 to 10.

Karyl Bannister

CHEESY BREAD

Wonderful with soup on a cold, snowy, winter day.

1 loaf bakery French bread
8-oz. pkg. sliced Swiss cheese
2 T. onion, chopped
1 T. dry mustard
1 T. poppy seed
1 t. seasoned salt
1 cup margarine, melted

Using a serrated bread knife, cut diagonal slits in the bread, going almost all the way through. Put the bread on a large piece of foil on a baking sheet. Place pieces of the Swiss cheese in the slits. Combine the last 5 ingredients and pour over the bread. Wrap the foil around the bread. Bake at 350 degrees for 35 to 40 minutes. Serve warm.

Tammy McCartney
Oxford, OH

Hope is one of those things in life you cannot do without. ~ LeRoy Douglas

Cookies, cookies,

Moist and chewy, thin and crispy, iced and decorated…you can never have too many holiday cookies! This year, why not invite your fellow cookie-lovers over for an old-fashioned cookie swap? Everyone bakes one kind of cookie, but goes home with a delicious variety. You'll find the tastiest refreshments among the yummy recipes on the following pages.

Here are a few ideas to get you started (clockwise from top left): Raspberry-Almond Squares, Pecan Munchies, iced with tinted Good and Glossy Cookie Frosting, German Chocolate Cake Mix Cookies, Cherry Bonbon Cookies,

COOKieS!

During the second week in December, before things get too hectic, I hold my annual cookie swap. I invite 25 friends, who each bake 10 dozen holiday cookies. We vote on the nicest-looking cookie...and even the saddest cookie! The winners get awards and we all have lots of laughs. All the women go home with a cookie cookbook that I have put together with all the recipes for the cookies. My family eats a lot of the cookies, but we also save some to put in pretty holiday tins that are given to people as little holiday remembrances.

— Barbara Leclair

Christmas Wreaths, Gingerbread Men (in basket and on plate), Yummy Marshmallow Bars, White Velvet Cut-Outs Candy Cane Cookies and Grandma's Soft Sugar Cookies. The recipes are on pages 100-103.

CHRISTMAS WREATHS

The next time your kids enjoy a "snow day," spend part of it making these quick and easy cookies.

3½ c. corn flake cereal
30 regular-size marshmallows
½ c. margarine
1 t. vanilla extract
2 t. green food coloring
Garnish: red cinnamon candies or
   maraschino cherries

Spread corn flake cereal on a baking sheet. Heat marshmallows, margarine, vanilla and food coloring in a double boiler until marshmallows melt. Carefully pour marshmallow mixture over cereal. Blend well and, as mixture cools, spoon 2 tablespoons of mixture onto wax paper. Form cereal mixture into a wreath shape. Arrange candies on top of each wreath to resemble holly berries. Allow wreaths to set up. Makes about 2 dozen.

Roxanne Bixby
West Franklin, NH

RASPBERRY-ALMOND SQUARES

These cookies are light and buttery. I especially enjoy them during the holidays because of the different flavor the raspberry jam gives them. Best of all, they are quick and easy to make.

1 c. butter, softened
1 c. sugar
1 egg
½ t. almond extract
2½ c. all-purpose flour
½ t. baking powder
¼ t. salt
⅔ c. raspberry jam, melted
½ c. slivered almonds, toasted

Preheat oven to 350 degrees. Beat butter and sugar with an electric mixer until light and fluffy. Beat in egg and almond extract. Add flour, baking powder and salt; beat until blended. Spread in an ungreased 9"x9" pan; smooth the surface. Spread jam on surface. Sprinkle almonds over jam. Bake 20 minutes or just until edges are golden. Cool, then cut into 1½-inch squares. Makes 3 dozen.

Theresa Smith

WHITE VELVET CUT-OUTS

We tinted Good and Glossy Cookie Frosting instead of the glaze to ice green, red and yellow Christmas balls.

Cookies:
1 c. butter, softened
3 oz. cream cheese, softened
1 c. sugar
1 egg yolk
½ t. vanilla extract
2½ c. all-purpose flour
sprinkles or colored sugar

Glaze:
1 c. powdered sugar
1 T. water
½ t. lemon juice

For cookies, cream butter and cream cheese together. Beat in sugar. Add egg yolk and vanilla, stir in flour. Shape dough into a ball. Wrap in plastic and chill overnight. To prepare, preheat oven to 350 degrees. On a lightly floured surface, roll out dough to ¼-inch thickness. Cut into 2½-inch circles or desired shapes. Place cookies on ungreased baking sheets. Bake for 12 minutes or until edges are golden. Cool on wire racks. Ice with glaze or with tinted Good and Glossy Cookie Frosting. For glaze, mix ingredients together and spread a thin coat on top of each cookie. Decorate cookies with colorful sprinkles or sugar. When glaze is dry, store cookies in an airtight container. Makes about 3 dozen.

Sharon Hill

Grandma's Soft Sugar Cookies

...Sweet memories of Grandmother's kitchen.

1½ c. sugar
1½ c. butter or margarine
1 c. flaked coconut
1 t. vanilla extract
1 egg
3 c. all-purpose flour
1 t. baking powder
½ t. salt

Mix sugar, butter, coconut, vanilla & egg together. Stir in remaining ingredients. Shape dough by rounded teaspoonfuls into balls. Place on ungreased baking sheet 3" apart. Flatten cookies to 2" in diameter with a glass dipped in sugar. Bake at 350° 'til cookies are set ~ about 7 to 9 minutes. Cookies will be pale in color. Cool slightly. Remove from baking sheet and store tightly covered. Makes 6 dozen.

The best way to clean metal cookie cutters is to carefully brush the crumbs away with a toothbrush. If you must use water, dry the cutters thoroughly to prevent rusting. Never wash them in the dishwasher!

The smiling gingerbread man on our sweet invitation provides a clue to the holiday fun to come! See page 130 for the surprisingly simple how-to's.

GINGERBREAD MEN

These fun fellows are always invited to cookie parties. Let the kids help dress them!

1 c. shortening
½ t. salt
3 t. baking soda
2 t. ground ginger
2 t. cinnamon
1 t. ground allspice
1 c. sugar
1 c. dark molasses
2 eggs, beaten
1 t. instant coffee granules, moistened with tap water
5 c. all-purpose flour
raisins, chocolate chips, sprinkles, colored sugar and candies

Cream together first 6 ingredients. Add sugar and molasses and continue to beat. Add beaten eggs, coffee and 3 or 4 cups of flour and continue to beat. Add remaining flour and mix by hand. (Dough will be very stiff.) Cover with plastic wrap and refrigerate for several hours or overnight. Flatten the dough on a floured board and cut out large and small gingerbread men with cookie cutters. Transfer to a baking sheet and use diced raisins, chocolate chips, sprinkles, sugar and candies to dress your gingerbread men. Bake at 325 degrees 10 to 13 minutes for small cookies and 15 to 20 minutes for large cookies. Makes 2 dozen small and 2 dozen large.

Good and Glossy Cookie Frosting

...SETS UP LIKE ROYAL ICING BUT WITH A GOOD & GLOSSY FINISH.

¼ c. WATER
1 T. LIGHT CORN SYRUP
3 c. PLUS 3 T. POWDERED SUGAR
½ t. CLEAR VANILLA EXTRACT

Combine water & corn syrup in heavy saucepan. Add sugar & blend well. Using a candy thermometer, cook over medium-low heat until temperature reaches 100° ~ stir constantly! Remove from heat & stir in vanilla. Cool for 5 to 8 minutes. Ice cookies. Stir icing occasionally. You can sprinkle on candy decorations, nonpareils & colored sugars before the icing hardens. (★ Replace vanilla extract with almond or lemon extract just for fun ~ and yumminess!)

YUMMY Marshmallow Bars

½ c. butter, softened
1 c. sugar
2 eggs
¾ c. all-purpose flour
2 T. baking cocoa
½ c. walnuts, chopped
1 T. vanilla extract
10.5-oz. pkg. mini marshmallows

Mix all ingredients except marshmallows together. Spread cookie mixture evenly in bottom of ungreased 13"x 9" pan. Bake at 350° for 15 to 20 minutes. Remove from oven & top with mini marshmallows. Return pan to oven & bake an additional 5 minutes or until marshmallows begin to melt. Cool in pan, then ice with...

CHOCOLATE FROSTING

1 c. SUGAR
½ c. MILK
¾ c. BUTTER
½ c. CHOCOLATE CHIPS

Mix sugar, milk & butter in a saucepan. Bring to a boil. Let boil for 1 minute. Reduce heat & stir in chocolate chips. Keep stirring 'til well blended & chocolate has melted. Cool, then spread on bars.

"Hang the merry garlands over all the town.
Smell the spicy odors of cookies turning brown!
The mice have come to nibble, they're feeling mighty gay —
But only little children shall have my sweets today!"

— Unknown

PECAN MUNCHIES

Every year before Thanksgiving, my mother managed to have at least 40 dozen cookies baked and in the freezer for the holidays! Of all her recipes, this is the one I like most.

1 c. pecans, chopped
1 c. butter, softened
½ c. powdered sugar
2 t. vanilla extract
1 T. water
2 c. all-purpose flour
6-oz. pkg. chocolate chips
Garnish: powdered sugar

Spread pecans in a single layer on a baking sheet and toast at 375 degrees for 5 minutes; watch carefully to avoid burning pecans. Set aside to cool. Cream the butter and powdered sugar together until light and fluffy. Add vanilla and beat again. Thoroughly mix in the water and flour, then add chocolate chips and pecans. Shape into small balls, approximately 2 teaspoons of dough each. Place on an ungreased baking sheet and bake at 300 degrees for about 20 minutes. While still warm, roll cookies in powdered sugar and place on cookie rack to cool. Makes 4 dozen.

Randi Daeger
Rockford, IL

GERMAN CHOCOLATE CAKE MIX COOKIES

These one-bowl cookies are quick and easy!

18¼-oz. German chocolate cake mix
1 c. semi-sweet chocolate chips
½ c. long-cooking oats, uncooked
½ c. raisins
½ c. oil
2 eggs, slightly beaten

Combine ingredients in a large bowl. Drop rounded teaspoonfuls of dough 2 inches apart onto ungreased baking sheets. Bake at 350 degrees 7 to 9 minutes or until cookie is set. Cool for one minute and remove from baking sheets. Makes 5½ dozen.

Ann Fehr
Collegeville, PA

CHERRY BONBON COOKIES

A family recipe that's over 30 years old.

24 maraschino cherries
1/2 c. margarine, softened
3/4 c. powdered sugar, sifted
1 1/2 c. all-purpose flour
1/8 t. salt
2 T. milk
1 t. vanilla extract

Drain cherries, reserving 1/4 cup of juice for glaze; set aside. Beat margarine until creamy. Gradually add powdered sugar, beating well. Stir in flour and salt. Add milk and vanilla; mix well. Shape into 24 balls. Press each ball around a cherry, covering it completely. Place on ungreased baking sheets. Bake at 350 degrees for 16 to 18 minutes. Transfer to wire racks and cool completely. Sprinkle with powdered sugar.

Cherry Glaze:
2 T. margarine, melted
2 c. powdered sugar, sifted
1/4 c. reserved cherry juice
1 to 2 drops red food coloring

Mix margarine, powdered sugar, cherry juice and food coloring. Place in a small plastic zipping bag and seal. To drizzle, snip a tiny hole at one corner of bag and gently squeeze over cookies.

Flo Burtnett
Gage, OK

CANDY CANE COOKIES

This brings back the old-fashioned fun of baking Christmas cookies.

1 c. butter, softened
1/2 c. brown sugar, packed
1/4 c. sugar
2 egg yolks
1 t. vanilla extract
1/2 t. peppermint extract
1/4 t. salt
2 1/2 c. all-purpose flour
red food coloring

Cream butter and sugars together; add egg yolks. Stir in extracts and set aside. Combine salt and flour; stir into sugar mixture. Divide dough in 2 equal portions and tint one portion red. Remove one tablespoon of dough from each bowl. On a very lightly floured surface, shape each tablespoon of dough by rolling under both hands to form a rope. Place the 2 ropes side-by-side and gently twist together. Carefully bend the top to form a candy cane; continue with remaining dough in each bowl. Place candy canes on an ungreased baking sheet, about one inch apart; bake at 350 degrees for 8 minutes. Do not brown. Let cool on baking sheet. Makes 2 dozen.

Candy Hannigan
Monument, CO

Remind each guest to bring copies of her cookie recipe to share…everyone can tuck their favorite recipes in the handy pocket on the take-home cookie sacks that they'll fill at your party. Instructions are on page 130.

WRAP IT UP!

Don't wrap your country gifts in just any old Christmas paper! Check out these clever packaging ideas…snippets of festive homespun make great bags, or use scraps of fabric, decorative paper or pieces cut from brown paper sacks to wrap packages…dress them up with torn-fabric "ribbon," colorful raffia or rick-rack. Finish your wrapping with one-of-a-kind tags, and you're all set!

Keep wrapping materials handy. Put paper, ribbon, tags, scissors and tape in a large basket next to the fireplace or under an end table. You'll be ready to lend a hand for last-minute wrapping projects.

For quick-and-easy gift tags: Use decorative-edge craft scissors to cut pictures from old greeting cards, then cut colored paper a little larger than the pictures and glue them together.

OH·
MY·AREN'T·YOU·
CLEVER
GIFT
WRAPS

from the Country Friends®

GIFT WRAP & TAG IDEAS

If it can be taped, sewn or glued, consider it for gift wrap...a piece of homespun, folded in half and sewn along the sides to make a bag, is an extra "gift" in itself! Use brown paper bags, scraps of fabrics, decorative paper, cellophane or whatever you have on hand to wrap the gift, then tie with raffia, ribbons or strips torn from fabric. Top off your presentation with small glass balls or a one-of-a-kind name tag tied onto the gift. You can use a photocopy of one of our tags from page 157, glue it onto card stock and cut it out. Color it with markers, crayons or colored pencils (don't forget to add small craft stick arms to the snowman). Mailing tags make quick gift tags! Handletter or use rubber stamps to add names and Christmas greetings.

You can transform plain brown or white paper into one-of-a-kind gift wrap! Use pre-cut holiday stencils or simple sponge shapes to paint on festive borders or scenes.

Christmas Customs

One of the things we love best about the holidays is keeping traditions, like placing candles in the windows and trimming an evergreen with ornaments and lights. You can create an updated version of the Yule log to use as a candleholder *(turn to page 130)**, or have a "family craft night" to make colorful decorations from paper and felt…they're sure to bring back favorite childhood memories!*

Did you know that the tradition of the Yule log goes back to a ritual practiced by the Vikings? As the winter solstice approached, they would burn a large log in the hopes of not only bringing light and warmth to the dark winter days, but also to ensure the return of summer by pleasing their sun god. Europeans who later adopted this custom would venture out on Christmas Eve in search of the perfect log from an apple or oak tree to bring home. It would then be blessed and placed in the fireplace to burn during the 12 days of Christmas. Today, few people burn Yule logs, but the tradition has been passed on in a symbolic form as we enjoy a Bûche de Nöel, or Christmas log cake. This delicious cream-filled cake, covered in chocolate frosting, is a sweet reminder of the very beginnings of this ancient tradition.

FOCUS ON **PeOPLe** INSTEAD OF ACTIVITIES & OBJECTS. SPEND SOME QUIET TIME WITH YOUR **FAMILY.**

Yarn Wreath

Cut a ring from cardboard. Wrap the ring with yarn, gluing the ends to secure. Add buttons, a yarn bow and a hanger to finish your festive adornment.

Felt Mitten Clip

Trace the pattern on page 153 onto tracing paper. Using the pattern, cut 4 mittens from felt. For each side of the clip, glue two mitten pieces together. Add rick-rack, sequins or other trims and sparkles to one mitten. Glue a mitten to each side of a spring-type hair clip or a clothespin. Use these cute clips on packages, the tree or to hang cards on the garland over the fireplace.

OLD-FASHIONED ORNAMENTS

Take a night out from your hectic holiday schedule to make holiday memories with your family...make one or all of these fun-for-kids ornaments to adorn your tree.

Paper Chain

Put some new twists on an old favorite...use decorative-edge scissors to cut out the strips, layer a narrow strip cut from decorative paper on top of the base strip and use rubber stamps to decorate some of the strips before you assemble your chain.

Paper Ball Ornaments

Cut 20 circles from paper (we used a huge circle cutter for scrapbooking and it went really fast). You can stamp some of the circles with Christmas stamps if you'd like. Fold in the edges of each circle to form a triangle. Now, start gluing! Glue the flaps of the circles together...pretty soon your ball will start to take shape. Don't forget to add a hanger before you glue the last piece in place.

We have all got our "good old days" tucked away inside our hearts, and we return to them in dreams like cats to favorite armchairs.

—BRIAN CARTER—

Yummy Little ♥ Gifts ♥

Need a bunch of little gifts for your friends, neighbors or teachers? Dress up plain mugs with simple hand-drawn designs and tuck in candy-coated pretzels for snacking, or share pretty little boxes filled with butter fudge. Our yummy beverage mixes and flavorful vanilla sugar are sure to warm hearts…and tickle tummies, too! See page 130 to paint the candy box.

PRETZEL WANDS

Delight your friends with this magical combination of sweet and salty flavors.

10 oz. vanilla candy coating
9-oz. pkg. large stick pretzels
(about 8½" long)
red and green mint candies,
crushed

Melt candy coating in a microwave-safe 2-cup measuring cup on high power (100%) one to 2 minutes, stirring every 30 seconds, until smooth. Dip each pretzel into candy coating to cover half of pretzel. Sprinkle with crushed candies. Stand each pretzel, coated side up, in a glass until candy coating hardens. Makes about 2 dozen.

The Manner of giving is worth More than the gift.
— Pierre Corneille

DESIGNER MUGS

Use a paint pen to draw "peppermint" swirls or a name and dots on a plain mug…add stripes around the handle if you wish. Fill the mug with goodies or treats and you have the perfect gift for your favorite snacker!

CHRISTMAS BUTTER FUDGE

An old-fashioned recipe that's perfect to share with your neighbors.

4 c. sugar
2 c. milk
1/2 c. butter
1/4 t. salt
1 t. vanilla extract
1/4 c. candied cherries, finely chopped
1/4 c. pistachios, blanched

Combine sugar, milk, butter and salt in large saucepan. Bring to a boil, stirring constantly until sugar is dissolved. Cook over medium heat, stirring occasionally, until candy thermometer reads 236 degrees. Remove from heat immediately; set pan in cold water. Do not stir or beat until cooled to lukewarm. Add vanilla; beat until candy becomes thick and creamy and loses its shine. When candy begins to set, add cherries and nuts; fold in quickly. Pour into buttered 8"x8" pan. Let stand at room temperature until firm. Cut into squares. Makes 2 1/2 pounds.

Juanita Williams
Jacksonville, OR

VaNiLLa SugaR
SO GOOD YOU'LL WANT TO SNEAK A PINCH

Place one or two whole vanilla beans with two cups of sugar in an airtight jar. Store in a cool place for about two weeks before using. Use in place of regular sugar in recipes, beverages or cereal.

Fix a jar full and tie on a pretty ribbon for someone with a sweet tooth.

FIRESIDE COFFEE MIX

Give this mix as part of a gift bag with some chocolate-covered spoons or cinnamon sticks, freshly grated nutmeg and a can of whipped cream!

2 c. hot chocolate mix
2 c. nondairy creamer
1 1/2 c. sugar
1 c. instant coffee granules
2 t. cinnamon
2 t. nutmeg

Blend together all ingredients and place in an airtight container. Include these instructions with your gift: For a single serving, place 2 tablespoons of mix in a mug, add one cup hot water and stir. Garnish with whipped cream and a sprinkling of nutmeg or cinnamon.

Lori Anderson
Eau Claire, WI

MULLING SPICE BAGS

Friends will think of you when they drink a mug of this spiced cider.

4 cinnamon sticks
8 whole allspice
8 whole cloves
4 T. dried orange peel
cheesecloth and
    butcher's twine

Cut a double thickness of cheesecloth into 4"x6" squares. Onto each square, place one cinnamon stick, 2 cloves, 2 allspice and one tablespoon orange peel; bundle up and tie with twine. To serve, place a spice bag in one gallon of cider. Simmer 30 minutes.

Jacqueline Lash-Idler
Rockaway, NJ

PUPPY CHOW SNACK MIX ...FOR PEOPLE!

For a tasty variation, use butterscotch chips in place of chocolate chips.

8 oz. bite-size crispy rice cereal
    squares
½ c. margarine
6-oz. pkg. chocolate chips
½ c. peanut butter
2 c. powdered sugar

Put cereal squares in a large bowl. Melt margarine, chocolate chips and peanut butter together. Pour over cereal squares and mix well. Put sugar in a paper bag; pour cereal mixture into bag and shake. Put finished snack into a plastic zipping bag.

Barb Agne
Deleware, OH

A yummy blend of chocolate and peanut butter, our Puppy Chow Snack Mix is meant for people! Instructions for the peek-a-boo gift bag are on page 130.

DECORATED JAR LABELS

Make a gift of your family favorite recipe extra-special this gift-giving season. Use one of our designs from page 157 (or create your own), then refer to *Making A Tag Or Label*, page 132, to make your labels. Glue or use double-stick tape to secure each label to a jar filled with a sampling of the tasty treat.

For a family gift, pack a variety of homemade snacks in a big ribbon-tied basket or colorful plastic pail...add a tag that says "Emergency Rations."

An old Yugoslavian custom is to bake bread on Christmas Eve for family and friends. What is so special about this bread? Before it's baked, a large gold coin is inserted inside, and when it's served, it's anyone's guess who will receive that special piece. Children especially enjoy this old-fashioned tradition!

SAVORY CHEESE COINS

These make good prizes for children when playing dreidel.

2 c. shredded sharp Cheddar
    cheese
1/2 c. butter, softened
1 c. all-purpose unbleached flour
2 T. dried, minced onion
1 t. Worcestershire sauce
1/8 t. cayenne pepper
Optional: sesame seeds

Combine all ingredients except sesame seeds in a medium bowl; mix well by hand or with a heavy-duty mixer until a dough is formed. Divide the dough in half; shape each half into a log about one inch in diameter and 12 inches long. If desired, roll in sesame seeds to coat. Wrap the logs in plastic and chill 3 to 4 hours or overnight. When logs are completely chilled, cut each log into 1/4-inch slices. Place on greased or coated baking sheets; bake at 375 degrees for 10 minutes. Remove coins from baking sheets to cool. Store in an airtight container. Makes about 8 dozen.

CHOCOLATE ANIMAL CRACKERS

An easy-to-make treat during the busy holiday season.

12-oz. pkg. chocolate chips
2 T. shortening
1 large box animal crackers
colored sugar sprinkles

Melt chocolate and shortening in pan. Stir until smooth. Dip animal crackers into chocolate, covering both sides. Lift out with fork. Place on wax paper. While still hot, top with sugar sprinkles. Allow to harden. Store in an airtight tin.

Judy Norris

For munchers on the go, pack Savory Cheese Coins in peppermint-striped tubes or fill little pails with Spiced Pecans. How-to's for the packaging are on page 130.

SPICED PECANS

Keep extras of these sweet-and-spicy snacks on hand...they go fast!

1/4 c. margarine
4 c. pecans
1 1/2 c. sugar
1 T. cinnamon
1 T. ground cloves
1 T. nutmeg

Melt margarine and add pecans. Cook and stir 20 minutes. Drain on paper towels. Mix remaining ingredients in plastic container. Add warm pecans and shake to coat. Spread on a baking sheet to cool completely. Store in an airtight container.

Kathy Bolyea
Naples, FL

PITA CRISPS

Easy to prepare ahead of time. Just store in an airtight container for snacking.

3 T. virgin olive oil
1 t. dried basil
1/2 t. sea salt (or coarse salt)
12-oz. pkg. pita pockets (about 5),
    cut into eighths

Preheat oven to 450 degrees. In mixing bowl, whisk together olive oil, basil and salt. Add pita pieces and toss to coat well. Spread the pita triangles in a single layer on baking sheets. Bake for 4 to 5 minutes or until crisp.

There's nothing nicer than giving (or receiving!) a handmade gift from the heart. Crafted from felt cut-outs, our frosty wall hanging and personalized stockings are quick & easy to assemble using simple embroidery stitches…no real sewing involved! Instructions for the wall hanging and stocking start on page 130.

The custom of hanging stockings from the mantel comes from a legend that tells of St. Nicholas tossing gold coins down the chimney of three sisters who needed dowries. The money fell into the sisters' stockings that happened to be hanging beside the fireplace to dry!

···thinks the mistletoe tradition is a fabulous idea.

···has at least one Christmas tree in every room.

···has her picture taken with Santa every single year.

Preserve "special" artwork from your preschooler with contact paper and hot glue a magnet on back for smaller projects. For larger masterpieces...buy your own mat and frame and give grandparents an "original." Your child will be very proud to give something he made and you know how excited grandparents will be!

— Denise Turner

Kids still get pleasure from the simple things...a box of crayons, colorful marbles, a jigsaw puzzle, stuffed animals, Raggedy Ann or Andy, classic adventure books or a train set. These never go out of style.

HOME FOR THE HOLIDAYS!

*"Christmas, my child, is love in action.
Every time we love, every time we give,
it's Christmas."*

— Dale Evans

PAINT CAN CANDLEHOLDER

Create custom candleholders out of
something unique...like a paint can! Be sure
to use a brand new paint can to avoid a fire
hazard. Paint the can your desired base
coat color, then follow the manufacturer's
instructions to add a crackle finish. Knot
a length of coordinating ribbon around the
can, then glue a miniature, framed Christmas
charm over the knot of the ribbon.

*Instructions for the quilt angel are on
page 131.*

May Peace and Plenty be the first To lift the latch on your door, and Happiness be guided to your house by the candle of Christmas.

— old blessing —

ADVENT BOX

Paint this brightly colored box to hold small treasures to be opened one drawer at a time from December 1st through Christmas…perfect for little ones anxiously waiting for the big day!

Remove the drawers from a 25-drawer organizer, then paint the organizer blue. Use a white paint pen to draw snowflakes and dots on the organizer. Tape colored paper to the inside front of each drawer, then use a paint pen to number the outside of the drawer. For each drawer pull, fold a 2" length of ribbon in half and glue the ends inside the drawer.

GOING HOME FOR THE HOLIDAYS IS GOOD FOR THE HEART ★ SURPRISE SOMEBODY SPECIAL!

HAPPY NEW YEAR!

Resolve to make your New Year's party the best ever! Pack a merrymaking kit for each guest and add colorful charms to help folks keep track of their glasses. For a sweet treat, we vote for ice-cream sundaes…you can tuck bottles of yummy chocolate and caramel sauce in fancy bags. How-to's are on page 131.

HOT FUDGE SAUCE
Keep an extra jar in the fridge for late-night snacks!

1/2 c. baking cocoa
1 c. sour cream
11/2 c. sugar
1 t. vanilla extract

Using a double boiler, stir all ingredients together and cook over simmering water for about an hour, stirring occasionally. Drizzle warm sauce over vanilla or coffee ice cream. Makes one pint.

CARAMEL SAUCE
Tastes great on pound cake, shortbread and ice cream.

1 c. brown sugar, packed
1/2 c. whipping cream
1/4 c. light corn syrup
1 T. butter
2 t. cinnamon

In a large saucepan, heat all ingredients to boiling, stirring constantly. Reduce heat and simmer, uncovered, for about 5 minutes. Makes 1 1/2 cups sauce.

*Sarina Quaderer
Friendship, WI*

NEW YEAR'S EVE KIT

3, 2, 1…Hats off to the New Year! Make sure everyone at your party is ready to celebrate with their own party kit. Start with a glitter-covered hat…wrap it with some star garland for extra pizzazz. Throw in a loud noisemaker, a streamer-popping cracker and lots of glittery confetti wrapped in colorful cellophane. Wrap it all in clear cellophane and tie it up with shiny ribbons, sparkling wired garland and shiny trims. Add a copy of the tag from page 135, trimmed in sequins, to finish it off.

celebrate!
WITH HAT & HORN
THE OLD YEAR'S DONE
A NEW YEAR'S BORN!

YUMMY BREAKFAST ROLLS

Quick to assemble and bake...so delicious to eat.

2 8-oz. tubes crescent rolls
2 8-oz. pkgs. cream cheese,
    softened
1¼ c. sugar, divided
1 t. vanilla extract
½ c. margarine, melted
1 t. cinnamon

Unroll one can of crescent rolls into the bottom of a 13"x9" pan. Don't press seams together! Mix cream cheese with one cup of sugar and vanilla; spread over rolls. Place second can of rolls over top. Pour on melted margarine and top with mixture of ¼ cup sugar and cinnamon. Bake for 30 minutes at 350 degrees.

Hazel Hayden

CHILE RELLENO PUFF

This recipe is excellent as a brunch dish. Serve with warmed flour tortillas or tortilla chips and salsa, crisp salad or a vegetable.

7-oz. can whole green chilies,
    drained and split
1 c. shredded Monterey Jack
    cheese
6 eggs, slightly beaten
¾ c. milk
1 T. all-purpose flour
1 t. baking powder
½ t. salt
1 c. shredded Cheddar cheese
2 T. fresh cilantro, chopped
4 green onions, chopped

Sauce:
8-oz. can tomato sauce
1 t. dried oregano
¼ c. salsa

In a lightly oiled 11"x7" baking dish, layer split chilies and Monterey Jack cheese. Combine eggs, milk, flour, baking powder and salt. Pour over chilies; top with Cheddar cheese. Bake at 350 degrees for 30 minutes or until puffed and browned. Heat combined tomato sauce, salsa and oregano 5 minutes. Spoon warm sauce over each serving of chile relleno puff. Sprinkle with cilantro and chopped green onions. Serves 6.

Nancie Gensler

Fun party favors: bundle gold-wrapped chocolate coins in squares of white tulle and tie closed with silver ribbon...a symbol for prosperity in the coming year!

Mild green chilies form a flavorful base for this cheesy Chile Relleno Puff. Top servings with warm, tomatoey salsa and serve for a midnight breakfast. Cut wedges of Yummy Breakfast Rolls...a creamy filling makes them especially good!

HOPPIN' JOHN

Hoppin' John is a traditional good luck dish popular in the South. Eating it on New Year's Day promises a prosperous and healthy New Year.

1 c. dried black-eyed peas
10 c. water, divided
6 slices bacon, cut up
³/₄ c. onion, chopped
1 stalk celery, chopped
1¹/₂ t. salt
³/₄ t. ground red pepper
1 c. long-grain rice, uncooked

Rinse peas and put in a large saucepan with 6 cups water. Bring to a boil and reduce heat to simmer for 2 minutes. Remove from heat, cover and let stand one hour. Drain and rinse. In same pan, cook bacon until crisp. Drain fat, reserving 3 tablespoons in pan. Add peas, 4 cups water, onion, celery, salt and red pepper. Bring to a boil, cover and reduce heat. Simmer 30 minutes. Add rice; cover and simmer 20 minutes longer until peas and rice are tender. Stir in bacon.

A good book is the best of friends, the same today and forever.
— Martin E. Tupper —

A GOOD BEGINNING MAKES A GOOD ENDING.
~old English Proverb

If you're short on time, you can use canned or frozen instead of dried black-eyed peas in Hoppin' John. It's a hearty side dish or main course!

Create a festive scene...decorate your New Year's table with clocks of every size and shape, candles and a sprinkling of confetti.

For a glittering centerpiece, fill a large, round glass bowl (such as a salad, punch or trifle bowl) with shiny gold and silver ornaments; wind little white fairy lights around and through the arrangement.

On New Year's Eve, I serve my family roast pork. A pig always roots forward, symbolizing going into the New Year, as opposed to a chicken, which scratches backwards. On New Year's Day, if the first person to enter our home is a male, we will have good luck throughout the coming year. Our "good-luck man" is then rewarded with a silver coin.

— Anne Legan

For Your Valentines

Send sweet sentiments to your valentines with handmade greetings. It's easy to decorate your own cards with stickers and ribbon…you can hand-write your message or use rubber stamps and colorful ink. Surprise a special someone with a heart-shaped brownie, or for quick little gifts, share candies in tiny decorated jars.

WINDOW TO MY HEART CARD

A handmade Valentine for that special person! Trace the patterns, page 157, onto tracing paper. Using the medium heart, cut one heart each from red card stock, clear cellophane and decorative paper. For the window, draw around the small heart on the red heart and cut out with decorative-edge scissors. Glue the cellophane heart to the back of red heart. Leaving an opening for filling, glue the decorative paper heart to the back of the red heart. Glue Valentine stickers to card stock, then trim close to the stickers. Fill the heart with the stickers and some paper confetti; glue the opening closed. Draw around the large heart on white card stock and cut out using craft scissors with large scallop blades; glue the filled heart to the white heart. Punch a 1/8" diameter hole in each scallop, then glue on a pretty bow.

CHOCOLATE-RASPBERRY BROWNIES

The raspberry filling makes these brownies really special. Bake in a pan that has 6 individual heart-shaped molds.

1 c. unsalted butter
5 sqs. unsweetened baking
    chocolate, chopped
2 c. sugar
4 eggs
2 t. vanilla extract
1¼ c. all-purpose flour
1 t. baking powder
½ t. salt
1 c. chopped walnuts, toasted
½ c. seedless raspberry jam

Melt butter and chocolate in heavy saucepan over low heat, stirring constantly until smooth. Remove from heat. Whisk in sugar, eggs and vanilla. Mix flour, baking powder and salt in a small bowl. Add to chocolate mixture; whisk to blend. Stir in nuts. For each brownie, spoon 3 tablespoons of batter into a greased ½-cup heart-shaped mold; smooth batter forming an indentation in center. Fill with 1 teaspoon jam. Spoon 2 tablespoons batter over jam; smooth batter. Bake brownies at 350 degrees for approximately 20 minutes, or until tester comes out clean. Cool in pan 5 minutes; transfer to a wire rack to cool completely. Makes about 14 brownies.

Susan Brzozowski
Ellicott City, MD

CANDY JARS

Great for the kids to take to school…these are fast and fun! Fill small food jars with pink, white and red Valentine candies. Top the jars with several squares of tissue paper tied with cotton string, then apply a sticker. Add a tag made from card stock that has been stamped or stickered with a Valentine greeting…see page 132 for helpful hints on Making Tags and Labels.

VALENTINE CARDS

Create custom cards! Start with a folded piece of card stock, then glue on a piece of decorative paper for the background. You can create a frosted overlay by attaching a piece of vellum with ribbon tied through holes in the top of the card. Add purchased tags with crimped ribbons (you can use a paper crimper to crimp satin ribbon), paper cut-outs, stickers and your Valentine message. Don't forget rubber stamps…they're perfect for quick & easy lettering.

INSTRUCTIONS

EGG TREE
(shown on page 10)

Begin by removing the contents from the eggs. For each egg, use a long needle to punch a hole in each end of an egg (slightly enlarge the hole in the pointed end) and to break the yolk. Holding the egg over a bowl and gently blowing into the smaller hole, blow the contents from the shell. Wash out the shells and allow to dry thoroughly.

Now to the fun part...dyeing the eggs! Apply self-adhesive hole reinforcements or use a craft glue stick to adhere silk leaves or flowers (with hard centers removed) randomly to the eggs; cover each egg with a piece cut from nylon stockings and tie to secure.

Make a dye bath for your eggs following the directions on an Easter egg dye kit. Immerse the eggs in the dye...you'll need to use a spoon to keep them from floating. Remove the eggs and allow them to dry thoroughly; remove the stocking covering and adhered shapes. Use paint or markers to add details to eggs as desired.

For each egg, tie a length of wired ribbon into a bow; glue the knot of the bow over the hole in the top of the egg. For the hanger, use a needle to thread clear nylon thread through the top of the bow; tie the ends of the thread together to form a hanging loop.

Glue jumbo rick-rack around the base of a wired tree. Hang the eggs on the tree...fill in empty spaces by gluing ribbon daisies to the tree here and there. Thread brightly colored buttons onto the branches as desired.

CHENILLE BUNNY
(shown on page 14)

Spring is just not Spring without rabbits to deliver Easter eggs. This rabbit will help with that job and he promises to not nibble on seedlings beginning to grow in the garden!

Use a ¼" seam allowance and match right sides unless otherwise indicated. Refer to Embroidery Stitches, page 133 before beginning project.

Trace the patterns, pages 135 and 136, onto tracing paper. Use the patterns to cut 2 heads, 2 ears and one carrot from white chenille. Cut 2 more ears from heavyweight fusible interfacing and 2 inner ears from striped chenille.

Pin the face pattern to the right side of one head piece. Using 6 strands of floss and working through the paper, work *Backstitches* for the mouth and *Satin Stitches* for the nose. Sew black shank buttons on the head for the eyes. Carefully tear away the pattern. For the whiskers, thread three 6-strand lengths of floss under the nose stitching; knot together to secure.

For each ear, fuse one piece of interfacing to the wrong side of one ear. Matching right sides and leaving the bottom of the ear open for turning, sew ear and inner ear together. Turn ear right-side out. Gather the bottom of ear, then sew to secure. Referring to Fig. 1, pin the ears at the top of the wrong side of the stitched head. Fold up the ears to keep them from getting caught in the stitching. Matching right sides and leaving an opening for turning, sew the head pieces together. Turn the head right-side out, stuff with fiberfill and sew the opening closed.

Fig. 1

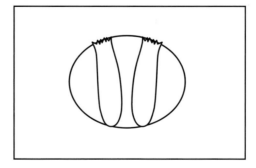

Matching right sides and leaving an opening for turning, sew the body pieces together. Turn the body right-side out, stuff with fiberfill and sew the opening closed. Sew the head and body together. Tack the feet to the head so the rabbit will stand.

Glue on a big, fluffy pom-pom tail; glue some silk flowers between the ears.

For the carrot, mix orange acrylic paint with water for a dye. Soak the carrot piece until it is orange; rinse and let dry. Matching right sides and leaving the top open for turning, fold the carrot piece in half and sew the edges together. Turn right-side out and stuff with fiberfill. Work *Running Stitches* along the top of the carrot; pull threads to gather, then knot thread ends together to secure. For the stem, cut a 2" square from green felt. Cutting to within ¼" from one edge and at ⅛" intervals, cut strips across the square. Roll the uncut edge and glue to secure; glue in end of carrot.

INDOOR BIRDHOUSES
(shown on page 16)

Embellish purchased wooden birdhouses into a home any bird would be pleased to live in...except these are for decorative purposes only!

To make the birdhouse with the "front door," apply primer, then ivory paint to a wooden birdhouse. Glue a rusted door plate to the front of the house, then glue a rusted skeleton key in the keyhole for a perch. Trimming to fit and wrapping over the edges of the roof, glue embossed wallpaper to the roof. Paint the roof brown...when the paint is dry, *Dry Brush*, page 134, the roof with ivory. Very lightly *Dry Brush* the raised pattern on the roof black. For a "balcony," glue an ornate drawer pull to the front edges of the roof.

For the green birdhouse, glue wooden drawer pulls to the bottom of the house for "feet." Paint the feet and roof ivory; paint the rest of the house green. Apply a light coat of wood-tone spray to the house and roof. Glue a decorative drawer pull plate above the door and a drawer pull below the door. Use a screw to attach a clear glass drawer pull in the hole in the plate. Paint a tree-shaped wooden finial brown, then glue it to the top of the roof.

GARDEN TOOL RACK AND FLOWER BOUQUET
(shown on page 20)

Turn a wrought-iron window unit into a handy collect-all for your gardening items.

For the rack, apply green paint to a wrought-iron window unit…use a piece of natural sponge to add rust-colored highlights while it's still wet. Paint metal buckets and wire baskets the desired colors, then rust them as above…we even found and painted a metal envelope-style container to hang. Apply clear spray sealer to the containers. Use jute to tie the painted items to the rack, then fill with gardening hand tools, gloves, seed packets or other small items…you can even fill one bucket with a bouquet of flowers you make yourself.

For the flowers, we gathered wooden star and snowflake cut-outs, candle cups, flowerpots and axle pegs. For each flower, place a pot or cup at the center of a star or snowflake, then drill a small hole through the center of each piece. Sand each piece and wipe with a tack cloth.

Use pliers to shape one end of a length of craft wire into a loop large enough to not slip through the holes. Thread the unlooped end of the wire through the inside of the pot or cup and through the star or snowflake (leave the end long for a stem); apply hot glue to the loop and, while glue is still melted, press a peg into the glue for a flower center.

Paint the flowers "springy" colors, and when the paint is dry, apply a coat of clear spray sealer. Wrap floral tape around the flower stems.

PAINTED POTS
(shown on page 20)

No garden is complete without flowerpots, and nothing perks up a patio better than one-of-a-kind pots!

Spray each clay pot and saucer with a coat of primer, then paint them with bright springtime colors. Use sponge brushes or spouncers to paint stripes, dots or flowers on some of the pots. Paint wavy lines, leaves, designs or sayings as desired. Apply 2 or 3 coats of clear acrylic spray sealer to the pots and saucers.

PAINTED BENCH
(shown on page 20)

When all is done, this bench will be a good resting place to admire your hard work in the garden.

Apply white primer to a wooden bench…maybe one you found at the flea market…then paint it with green exterior paint. After the bench is good and dry, refer to *Dry Brush*, page 134, to add a brown weathered look to the bench.

Apply 2 to 3 coats of clear sealer to the bench.

MOTHER'S DAY CARD
(shown on page 22)

What Mom wouldn't love something made especially for her? With this handmade card, you're bound to receive lots of smiles and maybe a hug or two!

Use a craft glue stick or spray adhesive to adhere coordinating decorative paper to the inside and outside of a blank card…you could use a 7"x10" piece of card stock for the card and just fold it in half.

Adhere a scalloped border sticker across the front of the card 1" from the bottom edge. Trim the card just below the border.

Glue petals from small white silk flowers to the front of the card…do not glue the edges of the petals down. Glue a button at the center of each flower. Cut leaves from decorative paper and glue them under the edges of the flowers.

For a message inside the card, use decorative-edge craft scissors to cut a rectangle from decorative paper. Use rubber stamps to stamp your message on the paper, then glue it inside the card.

Knot an 8" length of ribbon at the center. Notch the ends and glue the ribbon to the card.

MOTHER'S DAY PIN
(shown on page 23)

Have a fresh flower lapel pin ready to show off the sweet sentiment of flowers picked just for you from the yard. Simply attach a pin clasp to the back of a tiny perfume bottle using double-stick foam tape or household cement, then tie a ribbon around the neck. Now you're ready for unexpected gifts…you can also set it on the counter.

For a presentation card, use decorative-edge craft scissors to cut a rectangle from card stock large enough to accommodate the lapel pin and a message at the top. Use a permanent marker to draw a border around the card and write a message at the top of the card. Attach the pin to the card.

FLOWERING FIREPLACE SCREEN
(shown on page 26)

Use this planter to disguise the "black hole" in the fireplace during the warm-weather months.

Purchase a wooden window flower box to fit your fireplace opening; nail a length of picket fence to the back. (If you can't find a box to fit your fireplace, cut and nail 1"x8" lumber pieces together to form a box 8" deep.)

Paint the box and fence; when dry, *Dry Brush*, page 134, brown. Lightly sand the fence and box for an aged look.

Paint flowers, leaves, stems and scroll designs on the box. Apply clear acrylic sealer to the planter.

GET WELL BOOKMARK
(shown on page 29)

Layering colors of card stock and pieces of fabric, refer to *Making a Tag or Label*, page 132, to make a bookmark the desired size. (Ours measures 2³⁄₄"x7⁵⁄₈".) Punch a hole at the top of the bookmark, then adhere a colorful hole reinforcement. Use rubber stamps to stamp a message on the bookmark. Thread raffia through the hole and buttons onto the raffia, knotting raffia after each button. Place bookmark in a good book and present to an ailing friend.

FRIEND'S EMERGENCY KIT
(shown on page 30)

When a friend is sick, you want to do something nice for her. Why not fancy up a small suitcase and fill it with things to make her feel better? Note cards, a craft kit, puzzle books, hand lotion or a candle are all good things to include.

Allow paint and sealer to dry after each application.

(continued on page 124)

Apply masking tape to any hardware on the suitcase you do not want painted. Spray paint the suitcase…2 or more coats may be necessary for complete coverage. Paint the corners, then apply clear sealer to the suitcase.

Glue cute paper cut-outs, paper lace and silk flowers with pony bead centers on the suitcase as desired. Stamp catchy sayings and words of encouragement on the suitcase.

Gluing as you go, wrap the handle with ribbon.

CROSS-STITCHED BOUQUET
(shown on page 33)

Refer to Cross Stitch, page 132, before beginning project. Use the color key on page 142 for embroidery floss colors.

Using 3 strands of embroidery floss for the Cross Stitches, 2 strands of floss for the Quarter Stitches and 1 strand of floss for the Backstitches, work the design from page 142 at the center of a 7"x9" piece of 14-count white Aida. When your piece is stitched, frame it as desired.

FRIENDSHIP CALLING CARDS
(shown on page 33)

Whether meeting new friends or finding old ones, what better way to exchange phone numbers than with these fun and personal calling cards? With scrapbooking and rubber stamping so popular these days, you probably have most of the supplies already on hand! Refer to Making a Tag or Label, page 132, for general instructions and use pretty papers or fabric scraps, rubber stamps, markers or paint pens to help you create unique cards to fit your personality.

UNIQUE UTENSIL CATCHALL
(shown on page 35)

Sand the mailbox, if necessary, and wipe with a tack cloth. Apply primer, then white spray paint to the entire box, allowing it to dry after each application.

Make a color photocopy of a vintage tablecloth large enough to cover the mailbox. Using a thin layer of craft glue, adhere the photocopy to the mailbox; trim to fit. Apply clear acrylic sealer to the mailbox.

RECYCLED BENCHES
(shown on page 35)

No room in the house anymore for those old benches? Turn them into a shelf unit for the porch or sunroom.

Refer to Painting Techniques, page 134, before beginning project. Allow primer, paint and sealer to dry after each application.

Apply 2 to 3 coats of white primer to 2 wooden benches.

Enlarge the patterns on page 140 to fit your benches. Cut out all but the word patterns.

Apply repositional spray adhesive to the wrong side of the sun and cloud patterns, then adhere them to the bottom bench. Mix one part water with one part light blue paint. Using a stiff brush and randomly crisscrossing brushstrokes, apply paint mixture to benches…before the paint dries completely, use a paper towel to wipe some of the blue paint off until the desired amount of white shows.

Remove the patterns. Lightly Dry Brush the clouds blue.

Using the enlarged sun pattern and referring to Stenciling, page 134, make a sun stencil. Tape the stencil over the sun shape on the bench, then Sponge Paint the sun yellow. Use transfer paper to transfer the detail lines from the pattern to the painted sun and the words pattern to the front of the top bench. Sponge Paint orange cheeks on the sun; paint the words yellow. Use a black permanent fine-point marker to draw over the transferred lines and to randomly outline the words.

Apply 2 to 3 coats of matte clear acrylic sealer to the benches, then stack them for shelves.

SHUTTER BULLETIN BOARD
(shown on page 37)

- spray primer
- yellow, green and white acrylic paint
- paintbrushes
- wooden window frame
- 2 short wooden shutters
- leaf-shaped rubber stamp
- hardboard
- roll cork
- craft glue
- small nails
- 6 mending braces
- picture hanging kit

Allow primer, paint and sealer to dry after each application unless otherwise indicated.

1. Apply primer, then yellow paint to the frame and shutters. Using slightly thinned paint, stamp green leaves around the frame facing.

2. For a yellow wash, mix one part water with 2 parts yellow paint. Working in small sections, apply yellow wash to the frame and shutters; wipe immediately with a soft cloth. Repeat to make a white wash; apply to frame and shutters.

3. Cut a piece of hardboard to fit opening in frame. Cut 2 pieces of cork the same size as the hardboard piece. Glue one piece of cork to hardboard, then glue remaining cork piece to first cork piece. Secure hardboard in frame and nail in place.

4. With pieces right-side down on a flat surface, arrange shutters on each side of frame; use 3 mending braces on each side of frame to secure pieces together.

5. Follow manufacturer's instructions to attach hanging kit to back of frame.

MUNCHIE BOWLS
(shown on page 41)

Nothing could be better than a piping-hot bowl of popcorn…unless maybe the popcorn is served in a personalized bowl!

For each bowl, wash and dry an enamelware bowl thoroughly, then wipe with rubbing alcohol and allow to dry. Using alphabet rubber stamps and permanent enamel craft paint, stamp the desired name or message on the bowl. Paint sprinkles, swirls, dots, stars or hearts randomly on the bowl for an extra personal touch. Follow the paint manufacturer's instructions for drying and washing the bowl.

PATRIOTIC PORCH SWAG
(shown on page 42)

Show your American pride with this patriotic bunting for your front porch!

Press 5 yards of 45" wide patriotic fabric in half lengthwise; cut along the fold. (This will make 2 panels…each panel will make an 8-foot swag…sew one short end of each panel together for a really long panel.) Press each raw edge ½" to the wrong side and sew in place…press the top long edge of the panel 2" more to the wrong side and sew in place for a casing.

Using heavy-duty thread and leaving long thread ends at tops, work loose *Running Stitches, page 133*, across the panel every 36". Thread a hanging rod through the casing. To shape the swags, pull the long threads to gather the fabric; knot the threads to secure.

For each star accent, paint a wooden star cut-out white. Cut a 3" long piece of 16-gauge wire and staple one end to the back of the star. Shape the remaining end into a hook. Hang a star on the rod over each gather.

FLAG PIN
(shown on page 44)

Cut three 2¼"x3½" pieces from white fabric and one from batting. Fuse a piece of paper-backed fusible web to the wrong side of a scrap of blue fabric; cut out a 1¼"x2" blue field. Cut four 1¾" long and three 3½" long pieces of red rick-rack.

Place the batting piece between 2 of the fabric pieces and baste together ½" from the edges for the pin front. Aligning the top and bottom pieces just inside the basting lines and spacing evenly, sew the rick-rack pieces across the pin front; fuse the field to the top left corner inside basting. Using 6 strands of white embroidery floss, work *Cross Stitch, page 132*, stars on the field.

Matching edges and leaving an opening for turning, place remaining fabric piece on pin front and sew the pieces together just outside the basting lines. Turn the pin right-side out and remove basting stitches. Sew the opening closed; sew a pin clasp to the back.

STAR-SPANGLED TABLECLOTH AND FLOWERPOTS
(shown on page 44)

Tablecloth
Use the patterns on page 141 to cut star shapes from household sponges, then red and blue paint to *Sponge Paint, page 134*, stars onto a white tablecloth.

Flowerpots
For each pot, apply primer, then white paint to clay pot. Paint the rim of the pot

blue…when the blue is dry, use a small star-shaped sponge to *Sponge Paint* white stars around the rim. Paint red stripes down the pot below the rim…paint a thin yellow line on each side of each stripe and dots on the rim. Lightly sand the pot for an aged look, then wipe with a tack cloth. Apply 2 to 3 coats of clear acrylic sealer to the pot.

FRAMED STITCHED PIECES
(shown on page 50)

For each framed piece, trace the desired pattern from pages 142 or 143 onto tissue paper. Pin the pattern to broadcloth. Referring to the Stitching Key on page 142, work the indicated *Embroidery Stitches, page 133*, through the pattern. Carefully tear away the pattern. Refer to the photograph to add buttons to the stitched piece.

Mount the stitched piece in the opening of a pre-cut 8"x10" covered mat board with a 4"x6" opening. Mount the mat board in a wooden frame.

EMBROIDERED PILLOWS
(shown on page 50)

Match right sides and use a ¼" seam allowance for all sewing.

For each pillow, cut two 4½"x6½" strips, two 4½"x14½" strips and one 14½" square (back) piece from heavyweight fabric. Cut a 6½" square from hand-dyed muslin.

Trace the desired flower pattern from page 144 onto tissue paper. Pin the pattern at the center of the muslin piece. Working through the pattern and using 3 strands of embroidery floss, work *Backstitches, page 133*, along the pattern lines. Carefully tear away the pattern. Arrange and sew assorted white buttons to the flowers.

To make the front piece, sew the short strips at the top and bottom of the stitched muslin piece; sew the remaining strips to each side.

Place the front and back pieces together. Matching edges, pin jumbo rick-rack along the edges between the layers. Leaving one side open for turning, sew front and back together; turn right-side out. Place a 14" square pillow form in the pillow, then sew the opening closed.

CHEERY CHERRY APRON
(shown on page 53)

- 1⅔ yds. fabric for apron
- paper-backed fusible web
- red, green and brown fabric scraps
- black embroidery floss
- 4½ yds. jumbo rick-rack
- five ⅝" dia. buttons
- 14" of ⅝" wide ribbon
- safety pin

Use a ¼" seam allowance for all sewing and do all topstitching ⅛" from edge unless otherwise indicated.

1. Cut two 12"x13" bib pieces, two 4"x20" neck straps, a 4"x50" waistband and a 26"x45" skirt from fabric for apron.

2. Using the patterns on page 145 and referring to *Making Appliqués, page 133*, make one large and 2 small cherry appliqués from red fabric, 2 leaves from green fabric and one stem from brown fabric. Arranging stem, then cherries, then leaves, fuse appliqués to the right side of one bib piece. Referring to *Embroidery Stitches, page 133*, and using 3 strands of floss, work *Blanket Stitches* along the edges of the cherries and leaves and *Running Stitches* along the edges of the stem. Matching the edge of the rick-rack to the edge of the fabric, baste down the center of rick-rack along edges on the right side of the bib piece.

3. For each neck strap, matching right sides and long edges, fold strap in half, then sew long edges together; sew across one end and clip corner. Turn the straps right-side out and press. Refer to Fig. 1 to baste raw ends of straps to the bib piece.

Fig. 1

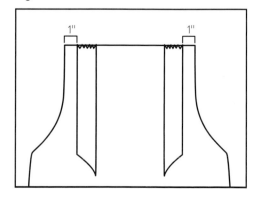

(continued on page 126)

4. Matching right sides and raw edges and leaving an opening for turning, sew remaining bib piece to appliquéd bib piece; turn right side out and sew opening closed.

5. Press the long edges of the waistband 1/4" to the wrong side. Matching right sides, fold the waistband in half lengthwise; sew across each end. Clip corners, then turn waistband right-side out. For apron placement, match ends, fold waistband in half and mark the center; unfold and mark 13" on each side of center mark.

6. For the skirt, cut gently-rounded bottom corners on the skirt piece. Press the bottom and side edges of the skirt 1/4" to the wrong side. Leaving half the width of the rick-rack extending past the fabric, pin rick-rack along pressed edges on wrong side of skirt; topstitch in place. Baste 1/8" and 1/4" from the top edge of the skirt; pull the threads to gather the skirt to 26" wide. Placing the skirt between the folds, pin the top of the skirt between the marks on the waistband. Topstitch along long edges of waistband.

7. Working on the front side of the bib, sew one button to each top corner of the bib. Centering the bottom of the bib on the waistband and matching bottom edges, sew 3 buttons, evenly spaced, across the bib to secure it to the waistband. Tie ribbon into a bow; pin between the leaves.

Pot Holder
- tracing paper
- quilted fabric
- red and green fabrics
- button

1. Trace the pot holder pattern from page 145 onto tracing paper. Use the pattern to cut one cherry each from quilted fabric and red fabric. Layer the pieces, wrong sides together.

2. Cut a 1 1/2"x23" bias strip from green fabric, piecing as necessary. Press one long edge, then one end of the strip 1/4" to the wrong side. Beginning with pressed end and matching raw edges, pin the strip to the red side of the pot holder; use a 1/4" seam allowance to sew strip to pot holder. Fold the pressed edge of the strip to the back of the pot holder and stitch in place.

3. For the hanging loop, cut a 1 1/2"x7" strip from green fabric. Matching wrong sides, press strip in half lengthwise and unfold, then press long edges to center; refold and topstitch along edges. Match short edges and sew together at an angle; trim seam. Sew the ends of the loop to the top front of the pot holder; sew a button over the ends.

Towel
Sew the ends of a 6" length of ribbon together to form a hanging loop. Sew the ends of the loop to the center of a dish towel…hang the towel by the ribbon loop from one button on the apron.

CHERRY CHAIR BACK COVER
(shown on page 54)

Large kitchen towels are the starters for this project…they'll fit the back of a standard kitchen chair. If your chair is wider, use 2 towels hemmed together along the long edges.

For the chair back design, cut an 8" square of print fabric. Working on the right side of the square and matching the edge of a length of rick-rack to the edge of the fabric, sew down the center of the rick-rack along all edges. Press the fabric edge to the wrong side so rick-rack extends along edges of square. Position the square on the bottom half on the right side of the towel; sew a button at each corner of the square to tack it to the towel.

Cut 2 strips from fabric 5" wide and 2 times the width of the towel. For each ruffle, matching right sides and long edges, fold one strip in half lengthwise, then sew across each end of the strip; clip the corners, turn right-side out and press. Baste along the raw edges of the strip, then pull the threads to gather the ruffle to fit the end of the towel. Pin the ruffle to the wrong side of one end of the towel, then sew in place. Repeat to sew remaining ruffle to opposite end of towel.

Matching wrong sides and short edges, fold the towel in half. With rick-rack extending along edges, pin jumbo rick-rack between towel side layers, then sew the side edges together, catching the rick-rack in the stitching.

CHERRY CHAIR CUSHION
(shown on page 54)

For all those long hours spent at the table crafting or just chatting, why not add a comfy seat cushion to make the time pass more comfortably?

To make a pattern for the cushion cover, draw around the chair seat on a piece of newsprint, then cut it out. Use the pattern to cut 2 cover pieces, 1" larger on all sides than the pattern, from fabric.

For each chair tie, cut a 3"x10" strip from a dish towel (we used one that matched our chair back cover). Matching right sides, fold tie in half lengthwise; using a 1/4" seam allowance, sew the long edges together. Turn the tie right-side out, then sew across each end.

Layer cover pieces, matching right sides and raw edges. Fold each chair tie in half; place one tie at each back corner between cover pieces, matching fold in tie with raw edges of cover pieces. Leaving a small opening for turning, sew the cover pieces together. Turn the cover right-side out, stuff with fiberfill and sew closed.

Sew hook and loop fasteners on opposite sides of the tie. Place the cushion on the chair and fasten the ties around the uprights to secure in place. Stack and glue 2 buttons together at the top end of each chair tie.

CASSEROLE COZY
(shown on page 60)

Deliver that special home-cooked dish in this super-soft dish cozy…a perfect housewarming or hostess gift!

For the cover, measure the length and width of your pan and add 4" to each measurement. Using the determined measurements, cut a piece of batting, a piece of fabric for the lining and a piece of fabric for the outside. Layer the fabric pieces, right sides together, then pin the batting piece on top of the fabric pieces; cut a 2" square from each corner.

Cut eight 4" lengths of ribbon. Pin one ribbon between the fabric layers at each outer corner…the long end of the ribbon should be inside the fabric stack, not sticking out the edges. Leaving an opening for turning and using a $1/4$" seam allowance, sew the pieces together; turn the cozy right-side out and sew the opening closed.

Glue a pretty trim or ribbon along the top edges of the cozy. Tie the ribbon together at each corner.

AUTUMN-PRINT LUNCHBOX
(shown on page 68)

- sandpaper
- metal lunchbox
- tack cloth
- masking tape
- spray primer
- light green spray paint
- natural sponges
- assorted acrylic paint in fall and metallic colors
- paintbrushes
- fall-motif rubber stamps
- toothpick
- clear acrylic sealer

Allow primer and paint to dry after each application.

1. If necessary, sand any rusted areas on the lunchbox, then wipe with a tack cloth. Mask the handle of the box if it doesn't need painting. Apply primer, then 2 coats of spray paint to the outside of the box. *Sponge Paint, page 134,* the rims with metallic paint.

2. Using a paintbrush, apply paint to the rubber stamp…layer colors to get a variegated imprint; stamp designs on the box for a sponge-painted look.

3. Use the toothpick to draw dotted tails from some of the leaves.

4. Apply 2 to 3 coats of clear acrylic sealer to the lunchbox.

5. Fill your newly crafted tote with goodies for a quick autumn picnic, a school ball game or just to be the envy of the lunch crowd!

TEACHER'S VEST
(shown on *page 69*)

Match right sides and use a $1/4$" seam allowance for all sewing unless otherwise indicated. Use 3 strands of floss and refer to Embroidery Stitches, page 133, for all stitching.

Start with a purchased denim vest with a straight bottom edge and a collar; remove the buttons from the vest. Measure the width of the bottom edge. Now, using the determined measurement as the length, cut two strips each from the following colors of fabric: $1^{1}/4$" wide green, 2" wide yellow, $1^{1}/4$" wide red and $5^{1}/2$" wide blue. Using the order above, sew the strips together along the long edges to make two fabric panels; press the seams to one side.

Working on the right side, sew a length of red jumbo rick-rack along the long raw edge of the green strip on each panel; press the seams to the wrong side.

Press the outer edge of each panel $1/4$" to the wrong side. If necessary, arrange and pin the panels on the vest to trim rounded corners to a $1/4$" seam allowance. Press the bottom and inner seam allowances $1/4$" to the wrong side. Arrange and pin the panels to the vest, then sew the outer, bottom and inner edges in place. Work *Running Stitches* along the top edges of the green and red strips and along both edges of the yellow strips. Work *Cross Stitches* over the red/blue seam, then work *Blanket Stitches* along the bottom and inner edges. Cut through the buttonholes that were covered and *Whip Stitch* fabric in place around the holes.

Trace the word patterns, page 141, onto tissue paper. Pin the patterns to the yellow strip, then work *Backstitches* over the words; carefully remove the paper. Work *French Knots* to dot each "i."

Using the star pattern, *page 141,* follow *Making Appliqués, page 133,* to make 2 stars. Fuse the stars to the vest. Work *Blanket Stitches* along the edges of the stars…stitch a *Running Stitch* tail from one point of each star.

Sew rick-rack to underside of collar along edges (half of rick-rack should extend past edge of collar), then work yellow *Running Stitches* along top edge of the collar. Replace buttons on vest with bright-colored buttons…sew buttons between the words.

HOT WATER BOTTLE COVER
(shown on page 70)
You can show your school pride (and stay warm) by using fleece in your team colors.

Cut eight $4^{1}/2$" squares from each color of fleece, two $8^{1}/2$"x$16^{1}/2$" pieces for the lining and one 3"x$8^{1}/2$" piece for the fringe.

Overlapping the edges $1/4$" and alternating colors, use a zigzag stitch to sew 4 squares together to form a row; make 4 rows. Repeat to sew 2 rows together to make 2 panels.

Matching right sides, sew a lining piece to each panel along one short edge; turn the panels right-side out.

Matching lining sides, place panels together. Pin $1/2$" of fringe piece between panels at bottom of cover. For a tie, fold a 24" length of $1/4$" diameter cotton cord in half. Pin fold of cord between panels, one square below the top at one edge of cover. Using a zigzag stitch, sew along side and bottom edges of cover. Make clips in fringe piece at $1/4$" intervals.

STADIUM BLANKET
(shown on page 71)

- $2^{1}/2$ yds. each of 2 colors of fleece
- rotary cutter and cutting mat

Sizes given in instructions will make a 50"x70" blanket. Overlap fleece $1/4$" and use a zigzag stitch for all sewing.

1. Cut seventeen $10^{1}/2$" squares from first color of fleece and eighteen $10^{1}/2$" squares from remaining fleece, then cut two 4"x50" and two 4"x70" borders from fleece.

2. Alternating colors, sew 7 squares together to make a strip. Alternating colors of first squares, make 4 more strips. Matching long edges, sew strips together.

3. Overlapping at corners, sew borders along edges of blanket. For fringe, clip borders at $1/4$" intervals.

JACK-'O-LANTERN PATCH

(shown on page 75)

Paint a wooden planter as desired and allow to dry; Dry Brush, page 134, with brown paint. Glue a miniature twig fence to the front of the planter. Trimming to fit, glue plastic foam blocks in the planter, then sheet moss over the foam.

For each Jack-'O-Lantern, cut a face from black paper and glue onto a miniature pumpkin. Glue the pumpkin to a stick from the yard. Tightly twist a long length of craft wire around the stem, pumpkin and stick several times to secure the pumpkin on the stick…curl the wire ends. "Plant" the pumpkin in the box.

Fill in around the pumpkins with more sticks and twigs. Cut some "leaves" from corrugated craft cardboard and glue randomly to the sticks and twigs.

For the sign, use a black paint pen to write "Happy Haunting!" on a small hanging wooden sign with a rusted tin plaque. Hang the sign from one of the twigs.

TOMATO COSTUME

(continued from page 79)

For the hat, trace the leaf pattern, page 147, onto tracing paper. Using pinking shears, cut 5 leaves and one 3¹/₂" diameter circle from green felt…you will also need to cut a 6"x12" rectangle for the stem and a 1"x30" strip for the ties. Glue the circle at the center of the tie strip. Glue a 6" length of pipe cleaner along one long edge of the stem felt piece. Tightly roll the felt around the pipe cleaner, then glue to secure. Glue one end of the stem to the center of the circle on the side with the tie strip. Pinching the leaf at the narrow section and gluing the pinched area to the circle, glue the leaves around the stem; bend the stem slightly.

BUG COSTUME

(shown on page 79)

- three colors of felt for wings and spots on romper, stripe down wings and spots on wings
- fabric glue
- knit romper
- fabric to match romper
- self-adhesive hook and loop fastener
- ¹/₂"w paper-backed fusible web tape
- three pairs of child-size socks

- polyester fiberfill
- safety pins
- heavy-duty thread and needle
- 2 pipe cleaners
- headband with spring antennae
- 2 pom-poms

1. Use a photocopier to enlarge wing pattern, page 148, to desired size…if necessary, cut the pattern apart and enlarge by sections, then tape enlarged copies together. Using enlarged pattern, cut wings, then 2 jumbo spots, 3 large spots, 2 medium spots and 5 small spots from felt for wings; cut 2 jumbo spots, 4 large spots, 4 medium spots and 10 small spots from felt for spots on wings. Cut stripe from remaining felt color.

2. Referring to the wing pattern for placement, glue the spots, stripe and hook and loop fastener on the wings. Referring to the front diagram, page 148, glue the spots on the front of the romper.

3. For each "extra" arm, measure length of romper sleeve from under arm to end of cuff; add 3¹/₂". Measure height of cuff; add 1". Cut a rectangle of fabric the determined measurements; use fusible tape to hem one short edge. Fuse a length of tape along one long edge on the right side of the fabric piece; remove the paper backing. Matching right sides, fuse long edges together; turn right-side out. Fold raw end up 1¹/₂" two times to make a cuff. Fill the toe of one sock with fiberfill. Insert the sock in the cuff end of the arm and glue to secure. Lightly stuff the arm and glue the opening closed.

4. Working from the inside of the romper, use safety pins to secure the arms to the romper…the arms should be close together. To make the arms move together, sew a length of heavy-duty thread between each arm…make sure it's long enough for the arms to hang slightly.

5. For each mitten, turn one sock wrong-side out. Cut a slit in the toe long and wide enough for the child's thumb. Use glue to "seam" the edges together, then allow to dry. Turn mitten right-side out.

6. For the antennae, insert a pipe cleaner in each spring of headband; trim even with end of spring. Wrap the remainder of pipe cleaners around springs. Glue a pom-pom to the end of each antenna.

LION COSTUME

(shown on page 78)

There's nothing cowardly about this lion! Turn a plain brown sweat suit into an adorable costume for a fall carnival…or just for playtime.

Trace the ear pattern from page 147 onto tracing paper; use the pattern to cut two ears from brown felt. Glue the ears to a plastic headband. Gluing as you go, make 8" long loops of yarn along the headband for the mane.

For the collar, measure around the child's neck and add 2". Cut a strip of felt 1" wide by the determined measurement. Apply self-adhesive hook and loop fasteners at opposite sides of the ends of the strips. Working on the same side of the strip with the rough piece of fastener, glue 8" long loops of yarn along the strip. Repeat to make wristbands.

For the tail, cut a 7"x23" piece of beige felt. Glue the long edges together to form a tube; turn right-side out. Wrap yarn around a 5" square piece of cardboard…wrap lots of yarn for a fuller tail. Tightly knot a length of yarn around the yarn at one end of the cardboard; cut the yarn at opposite end. Tie a length of yarn around tassel near top. Glue top of tassel inside one end of tail. Stuff tail with fiberfill and pin to pants.

Glue an oval of beige felt to the front of the shirt.

FAIRY COSTUME

(shown on page 78)

Use pinking shears for all cutting and allow paint to dry after each application.

- sheer fabric for capelet, collar and hat
- thumbtack
- string
- pinking shears
- assorted colors of dimensional paint
- small self-adhesive acrylic jewels
- ¹/₈" wide satin ribbon
- elastic thread
- 2 pipe cleaners
- hot glue gun
- plastic headband
- paintbrush
- gold glitter paint

128

1. For the capelet, measure the child from the back of the neck to the wrist; double the measurement. Cut a square of fabric the determined measurement.

2. To determine inside cutting line measurement, measure around child's head; divide measurement by 4. Using determined measurement for inside cutting line and original neck to wrist measurement for outside cutting line, follow *Making A Fabric Circle*, page 132, to cut out capelet.

3. Working 2¹/₂" from the outer edge and spacing evenly, pin desired number of photocopies of the circle design, page 148, to wrong side of the capelet...the design should show through to the right side. Using dimensional paint and working on the right side of the capelet, randomly draw stars in the upper area of the capelet; press an acrylic jewel in the center of each star. Make dots of paint over each circle design, then draw short, wavy lines along the outer edge.

4. For the collar, cut a 3"x24" strip of fabric. Use dimensional paint to draw wavy lines and stars along one long edge; attach one jewel to the center of each star. Using ribbon, work *Running Stitches*, page 133, along opposite edge.

5. Cut an 18" square from fabric. Using 9" as the outer cutting line and no inner cutting line, follow *Making A Fabric Circle* to cut out hat piece. Use dimensional paint to draw wavy lines along edge and random stars on hat. Using elastic thread, work *Running Stitches* 2" in from edge. Gather hat to fit head and knot ends on inside of hat.

6. For antennae, coil one end of each pipe cleaner and glue to headband; wrap ends around finger to curl. Brush headband and antenna with gold glitter paint.

DECORATED CANDLES
(shown on page 83)

Candles, candles everywhere...is there such a thing as too many candles?

For some of your candles, use corrugated craft cardboard (and decorative paper if you desire) to make a sleeve for the candle...tie it on with raffia or ribbon. You could even add a tag embellished with a metal charm.

For a vintage look, try covering pillar candles with grains and spices from the kitchen. First, cover a large work area with newspaper. Next, melt wax to coordinate with the color of your candle in a coffee can that has been placed in an electric skillet filled with water and heated to a boil. After the wax is melted, stir your favorite spices into the mixture. Use a 1" wide paintbrush to apply the wax mixture to the candle.

To add texture to the candle, spread a layer of uncooked oatmeal or bran on aluminum foil...apply wax mixture to the candle, then immediately roll the candle in the grain. Repeat, layering the wax mixture and rolling in grain until you achieve the desired results...it is not necessary to allow the mixture to dry between applications. Allow the wax to harden before lighting candle.

"THANKS" WALL HANGING
(shown on page 86)

- black, grey and coordinating colors of embroidery floss
- 15"x27" piece of 7-ct. Klostern
- paper-backed fusible web
- assorted felt

1. Using 6 strands of black floss and following the diagram on page 150, center and *Cross Stitch*, page 132, the words on the Klostern.

2. Using the patterns, pages 150 and 151, follow *Making Appliqués*, page 133, to make one appliqué of each shape from felt.

3. Referring to photograph, arrange and fuse appliqués on wall hanging. Using 2 strands of coordinating floss and referring to *Embroidery Stitches*, page 133, work desired stitches around, and detail stitches on, the appliqués. Use 6 strands of grey floss to work a *Cross Stitch* sidewalk.

4. Frame piece as desired.

STITCHED BREAD CLOTH
(shown on page 87)

This fall-motif bread cloth is the perfect compliment to your baked goods.

Using the patterns, page 149, and following *Making Appliqués*, page 133, make pumpkin, stem and leaf appliqués from fabrics.

Arrange and fuse the appliqués on one corner of a muslin bread cloth. Using 3 strands of embroidery floss, work your favorite *Embroidery Stitches*, page 133, to embellish the appliqués. Work *Running Stitches* along the edges of the cloth.

LEAF PLACEMAT
(shown on page 87)

Refer to Embroidery Stitches, page 133, before beginning project.

For each placemat, cut two 13"x21" pieces of fabric. Matching right sides, leaving an opening for turning and using a ¹/₂" seam allowance, sew fabric pieces together; turn right-side out and press. Topstitch pieces ¹/₂" from the edges.

For the leaf napkin holder, fuse the wrong sides of two 7"x10" pieces of fabric together. Enlarge the leaf pattern on page 151 by 125%; use the pattern to cut a leaf from the fused fabric. Stitch "veins" on the leaf. Use 3 strands of embroidery floss to work *Blanket Stitches* along the edges of the leaf. Pin the leaf on the placemat...put a napkin in it to gauge spacing. Stitch a straight line on the leaf on each side of the napkin. Sew a large button to the leaf.

For the nametag, use pinking shears to cut a 2"x4" piece from felt. Use embroidery floss to work *Running Stitches* along the edges. Cut a buttonhole at one end to fit the button on the leaf. Lightly draw the name on the tag, then use floss to work *Backstitches* over the drawn lines. Button the tag on the leaf.

COLLECTOR'S SHELF
(shown on page 92)

If you can't find an antique-looking shelf already made, they're really easy to make. Start with a piece of 1"x4" lumber the desired length for your backboard. Nail a piece of 1" thick rounded molding along the bottom and a piece of crown molding along the top (we mitered and beveled the corners on some of our lumber). Cut a piece of 1"x6" lumber for the shelf and nail it on top of the crown molding. Stain the shelf, then add heavy-duty hangers to the back.

(continued on page 130)

Use a photocopier to enlarge the patterns on page 152 to fit your backboard. Use transfer paper to transfer the words to the backboard. Referring to *Painting Techniques*, page 134, paint the letters. Paint a thin outline around each letter, then randomly outline the outlines in a few places. Shade the left half of each letter outside of the outlines brown. Apply stain to the bottom half of the letters and immediately wipe away with a soft cloth.

COOKIE EXCHANGE INVITATIONS
(shown on page 101)

For each invitation, cut a 7"x10" card from card stock; matching short edges, fold card in half. Cut a 4³/₄"x6¹/₂" overlay from vellum; use decorative-edge craft scissors to cut a background from decorative paper the same size. Use a permanent marker to draw over the word pattern, page 153, on the vellum. Using a craft glue stick, adhere the edges of the background, then the overlay, to the front of the card.

Trace the gingerbread man and heart patterns, page 153, onto tracing paper. Use the patterns to cut 2 hearts from fabric and a gingerbread man from card stock. Use a fine-point marker to draw a face and a red colored pencil to draw cheeks on the gingerbread man. Glue the gingerbread man to the front of the card; layer the hearts and glue them to the gingerbread man.

GINGERBREAD MAN TREAT BAGS
(shown on page 103)

Make one of these adorable bags for each guest at your cookie exchange party to carry home samples from the party.

Cut a 3¹/₂"x5¹/₂" piece from card stock for a pocket; glue sides and bottom of the pocket to the front of a decorative lunch-size paper bag. Trace the gingerbread man and heart patterns, page 153, onto tracing paper. Use the patterns to cut one gingerbread man from card stock, 2 hearts from fabric and one heart from batting. Glue the gingerbread man to white card stock; leaving a ¹/₄" border, use decorative-edge craft scissors to cut out gingerbread man.

Glue batting heart between 2 fabric hearts. Glue the heart to the gingerbread man. Use a fine-point marker to draw a face and a red colored pencil to draw cheeks on the gingerbread man...draw a black zigzag line along the edges of the pocket.

Cut a 3"x4¹/₂" card from red & white striped decorative paper. Matching bottom edges, glue it to a blank 3"x5" card; write desired recipe on the card, then tuck it into the pocket.

Fill the bag with treats. Fold the top of the bag 1" to the wrong side. Punch two holes at the top center of the bag through the fold...use a strand or 2 of raffia to tie the bag closed.

YULE LOG
(shown on page 106)

Making sure your log sits flat to avoid a fire hazard, drill holes in a log to fit your candles. Place the candles, then arrange fresh greenery around them.

PAINTED BOX
(shown on page 109)

Apply primer, then light blue paint to the outside of a small round paper maché box and lid; allow to dry. Apply self-adhesive snowflake-shaped stickers to the box.

For the knob, stack and glue several white buttons to the lid.

SNACK BAG
(shown on page 110)

Turn a plain colored lunch bag into a cute peek-a-boo bag for presenting a gift of snack mix to your friend.

Cut a square from the front of the bag. Cut a piece of clear cellophane and decorative paper 2" larger on all sides than the opening; glue cellophane inside the bag, covering the opening.

For the frame, cut an opening in the decorative paper slightly smaller than the opening in the bag...use decorative-edge craft scissors to trim the outside edges. Glue the frame to the front of the bag.

Glue a 1¹/₂" wide strip of decorative paper, trimmed with decorative-edge craft scissors, along the flap. Glue a length of grosgrain ribbon along the top of the strip.

Glue a large fabric-covered button to the flap. Hang a rubber-stamped tag from the button.

DECORATED BUCKET
(shown on page 111)

Cover a metal sap bucket with self-adhesive felt...trim the top and bottom edges even with the bucket.

Use decorative-edge craft scissors to cut a vintage Christmasy motif from a postcard or greeting card. Glue the motif to a piece of felt; use craft scissors to trim the felt ¹/₄" larger on all sides than the motif. Glue the motif to the front of the bucket.

Place your gift in cellophane and tie it closed with ribbon. Tie on a tag embellished with decorative paper and a Christmas charm. Place gift in bucket.

CANDY-STRIPED POPPER
(shown on page 111)

Use this unique gift wrap to keep them guessing what's inside!

Wrap a paper towel tube with white paper...glue the seam to secure; tuck the extra paper inside the ends of the tube. Gluing the ribbon ends inside the ends of the tube, spiral lengths of ribbons around the tube. Place gift inside tube, then fill the ends with tissue paper. Wrap the tube in cellophane and tie the ends closed with raffia.

Cut a tag from card stock; glue to a piece of decorative paper, then trim the paper ¹/₈" larger than the tag. Punch a hole in the tag; apply a self-adhesive hole reinforcement to the hole. Write a message on the tag; attach the tag to the raffia.

SNOWMAN WALL HANGING
(shown on page 112)

- tracing paper
- polyester batting
- orange and black felt
- ³/₄"x3¹/₂" yellow fabric for hatband
- 15¹/₄"x15¹/₂" piece of blue felt
- white, black and yellow embroidery floss
- 2 black snaps
- tissue paper
- 16¹/₄"x19" piece of red felt
- fabric glue
- buttons for holly berries
- artificial holly leaves

Refer to Embroidery Stitches. page 133, before beginning project. Use 6 strands of floss for all stitching.

1. Trace the patterns on page 155 onto tracing paper. Using the patterns, cut head from batting, nose from orange felt, hat from black felt and hatband from fabric. Arrange and pin head, hat and hatband on blue felt; pin nose on head. Work *Running Stitches* around head, hat, hatband and nose.

2. Work *French Knots* for the snowman's mouth; sew on snaps for eyes.

3. Trace the letter patterns, pages 154 and 155, onto tissue paper; trace another E and R. Arrange and pin the letters on the blue felt; cut out the letters. Center and pin the blue felt 3" below the top edge of the red felt. Work *Running Stitches* along the edges of each letter and the outside edges of the blue felt.

4. Use white floss to work *French Knot* and *Straight Stitch* "snowflakes" on the blue felt.

5. For the hanging sleeve, press the top edge of the red felt piece 2½" to the back; glue edge to secure. Glue buttons and leaves to the hatband.

CHRISTMAS STOCKINGS
(shown on page 113)

Stockings are fun for everyone to make. Whether making easy felt stockings or fabric stockings, you can use the pattern on page 156 as your starting place.

Basic Felt Stocking
Trace the stocking pattern onto tracing paper. Using the pattern, cut 2 stocking pieces from felt...cut out one heel and one toe shape if desired. If you're adding a heel and toe, pin them on one stocking piece and work *Blanket Stitches*, page 133, along the inner edges. Pin the stocking pieces together and use *Blanket Stitches* or *Running Stitches*, page 133, to sew them together.

For the cuff, cut a 4"x11½" strip from contrasting felt. Overlapping ends at back, glue one long edge of the cuff around the top of the stocking; fold the cuff down.

Basic Fabric Stocking
Use a ½" seam allowance for all sewing.

Trace the stocking pattern onto tracing paper. Using the pattern, cut 2 stocking pieces from fabric and 2 stocking pieces from lining. Matching right sides and leaving the top open, sew the stocking pieces together; repeat for the lining.

Cut an 8"x12" piece of fabric for the cuff. Matching right sides, sew the short ends together. Matching wrong sides and raw edges, fold the cuff in half.

Turn the stocking only right-side out and place the lining in the stocking. Matching raw edges and the seam of the cuff to the heel-side seam of the stocking, pin the cuff in the lining. Sew all pieces together along the top edge, then turn the cuff out.

Embellishing the Stockings
Buttons, beads and sequins can be glued or sewn on; appliqués can be glued, fused or sewn. If you want professional-looking letters, try some of the fonts from your computer for your patterns. Computer clipart, picture books and coloring books are great places to find patterns for trees, snowflakes and other Christmas motifs. Once you've found your pattern, cut the shapes from fabric or felt (refer to *Making Appliqués*, page 133, to make fusible appliqués) and start decorating.

QUILT PIECE ANGEL
(shown on page 114)

Made from a well-loved quilt, this angel can keep watch over a special friend.

Refer to *Embroidery Stitches, page 133*, before beginning project.

Trace the patterns, page 157, onto tracing paper. Using the body patterns, cut 2 bodies from an old quilt, 2 wings from cotton batting and one head from muslin. Sew a button to one body piece...this will be the front. Leaving an opening for stuffing, work *Blanket Stitches* along the edges of the body pieces to sew them together; lightly stuff with polyester fiberfill and sew the opening closed. Work *Running Stitches* along the edges of the wings to sew them together.

For the head, make a *French Knot* for each eye and a *Straight Stitch* for the mouth at the center of the muslin circle. Using a 1⅛" diameter covered button kit, cover the button with the embroidered head. Gluing to secure, encircle the head with a "halo" of small, pliable twigs. Sew the head to the top of the body and the wings to the back. Glue a small piece of trim to the neck for a collar. Hang several charms from the button.

GLASS CHARMS
(shown on page 116)

Never mix up glasses at a large gathering again...these fun charms make each glass unique!

For each charm, cut a 6" length of craft wire...if your stemware is larger than standard, you will need to adjust the length of your wire. Use needle-nose pliers to shape a small loop in one end of the wire; wrap wire around itself to secure. Thread beads onto the wire to within 1" from the end of the wire; place the beaded wire around the stem to make sure it fits. Twist the end of the wire around itself above the last bead to form a loop; flatten the loop, then bend the opposite end to make a hook.

To make the dangle, hook a 3" length of wire around the wire between 2 beads on the beaded circle. Thread beads onto the wire, then coil the end to secure.

BOTTLE BAG
(shown on page 116)

- two 7"x16" pieces of fabric for outer bag
- two 7"x16" pieces of fabric for lining
- ruffle trim for top of bag
- satin ribbon

Use a ½" seam allowance for all sewing unless otherwise indicated.

1. Matching right sides, sew long edges of outer fabric pieces together to form a tube. Repeat using lining fabric pieces. Turn liner right-side out.

2. Matching raw edges, pin ruffled trim along top edge of liner; baste in place.

3. Matching top edges and side seams, place liner in outer tube; sew around top edge, joining liner and tube. Pull the liner out and fold it over the outer tube. Flatten the bag...the bag will be inside-out with the bottom edge open; sew across the bottom edge.

4. To make a flat bottom, match each side seam to bottom fold line; sew across each corner 1½" from point. Clip corners and turn the bag right-side out.

5. Place bottle in bag, tie with ribbon and fold top of bag down to show lining.

GENERAL INSTRUCTIONS

CROSS STITCH

Counted Cross Stitch (X): Work one Cross Stitch to correspond to each colored square in chart. For horizontal rows, work stitches in two journeys (Fig. 1).

Fig. 1

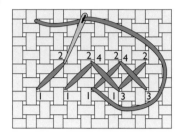

For vertical rows, complete stitch as shown in Fig. 2.

Fig. 2

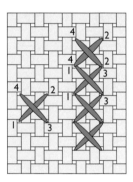

Backstitch (B'ST): For outline detail, Backstitch (shown in chart and color key by black or colored straight lines) should be worked after all Cross Stitch has been completed (Fig. 3).

Fig. 3

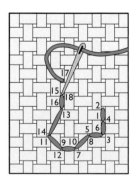

French Knot: Referring to Fig. 4, bring needle up at 1. Wrap floss once around needle and insert needle at 2, holding end of floss with non-stitching fingers.

Fig. 4

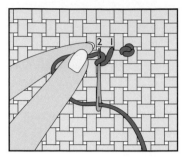

Quarter Stitch: Quarter Stitches are shown as triangular shapes of color in chart and color key. Come up at 1, then split fabric thread to take needle down at 2 (Fig. 5).

Fig. 5

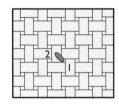

MAKING A FABRIC CIRCLE

1. Cut a square of fabric the size indicated in project instructions.

2. Matching right sides, fold fabric square in half from top to bottom and again from left to right.

3. Tie one end of string to a pencil or fabric marking pen. Measuring from pencil, insert a thumbtack through string at length indicated in project instructions. Insert thumbtack through folded corner of fabric. Holding tack in place and keeping string taut, mark cutting line (Fig. 1).

Fig. 1

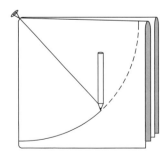

4. Cut along drawn line through all fabric layers.

MAKING PATTERNS

When the entire pattern is shown, place tracing paper over the pattern and draw over lines. For a more durable pattern, use a permanent marker to draw over pattern on stencil plastic.

When patterns are stacked or over-lapped, place tracing paper over the pattern and follow a single colored line to trace the pattern. Repeat to trace each pattern separately onto tracing paper.

When tracing a two-part pattern, draw over the first part of the pattern onto tracing paper, then match the dashed lines and arrows and draw over the second part of the pattern.

When only half of the pattern is shown (indicated by a solid blue line on pattern), fold tracing paper in half. Place the fold along the solid blue line and trace pattern half; turn folded paper over and draw over the traced lines on the remaining side. Unfold the pattern.

MAKING A TAG OR LABEL

For a quick and easy tag or label, photocopy or trace (use transfer paper to transfer design) a copyright-free design onto card stock...or just cut a shape from card stock.

Color tag with colored pencils, crayons or thinned acrylic paint; draw over transferred lines using permanent markers or paint pens. Use straight-edge or decorative-edge craft scissors to cut out tag; glue to colored or decorative paper or card stock, then cut tag out, leaving a border around it.

Use a pen or marker to write a message on the tag. You can also choose items from a wide variety of self-adhesive stickers, borders or frames; rubber stamps and inkpads; or gel pens in an assortment of colors, densities and point-widths, to further embellish your tags or labels.

EMBROIDERY STITCHES

Preparing floss: If your project will be laundered, soak floss in a mixture of one cup water and one tablespoon vinegar for a few minutes and allow to dry before using to prevent colors from bleeding or fading.

Backstitch: Referring to Fig. 1, bring needle up at 1; go down at 2; bring up at 3 and pull through. For next stitch, insert needle at 1; bring up at 4 and pull through.

Fig. 1

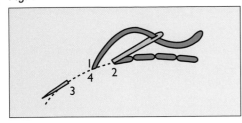

Blanket Stitch: Referring to Fig. 2a, bring needle up at 1. Keeping thread below point of needle, go down at 2 and come up at 3. Continue working as shown in Fig. 2b.

Fig. 2a

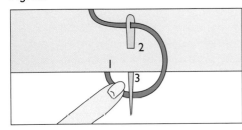

Fig. 2b

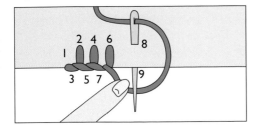

Cross Stitch: Bring needle up at 1 and go down at 2. Come up at 3 and go down at 4 (Fig. 3).

Fig. 3

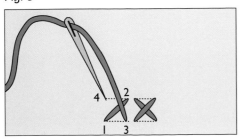

French Knot: Referring to Fig. 4, bring needle up at 1. Wrap floss once around needle and insert needle at 2, holding end of floss with non-stitching fingers.

Fig. 4

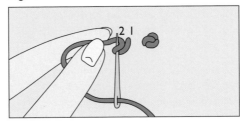

Outline Stitch: Come up at 1. Keeping thread below the stitching line, go down at 2 and come up at 3. Go down at 4 and come up at 5 (Fig. 5).

Fig.5

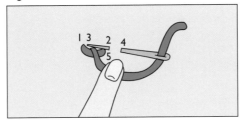

Running Stitch: Referring to Fig. 6, make a series of straight stitches with stitch length equal to the space between stitches.

Fig. 6

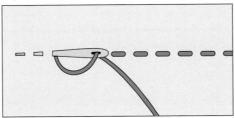

Satin Stitch: Referring to Fig. 7, come up at odd numbers and go down at even numbers with the stitches touching but not overlapping.

Fig. 7

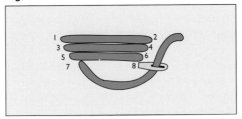

Straight Stitch: Referring to Fig. 8, come up at 1 and go down at 2.

Fig. 8

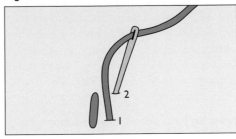

Whip Stitch: With right sides of folded fabric edges together, bring needle up at 1; take thread around edge of fabric and bring needle up at 2. Continue stitching along edge of fabric.

Fig. 9

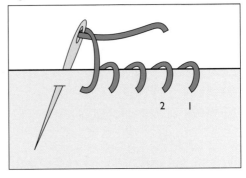

MAKING APPLIQUÉS

To prevent darker fabrics from showing through, white or light-colored fabrics may need to be lined with fusible interfacing before being fused.

To make reverse appliqués, trace the pattern onto tracing paper; turn traced paper over and continue to follow all steps using the reversed pattern.

1. Trace the pattern onto paper side of fusible web as many times as indicated in project instructions. When making more than one appliqué, leave at least 1" between shapes.

2. Cut out shape ½" outside of drawn lines. Fuse the shape to the wrong side of fabric, then cut out along drawn lines.

PAINTING TECHNIQUES

Transferring a pattern: Trace pattern onto tracing paper. Place transfer paper, coated side down, between project and traced pattern. Use removable tape to secure pattern to project. Use a pencil to draw over outlines of design (press lightly to avoid smudges and heavy lines that are difficult to cover). If necessary, use a soft eraser to remove any smudges.

Painting base coats: Use a medium round brush for large areas and a small round brush for small areas. Do not overload brush. Allowing to dry between coats, apply several thin coats of paint as needed for desired coverage.

Transferring details: To transfer detail lines to design, reposition pattern and transfer paper over painted base coats and use a pencil to lightly draw over detail lines of design.

Adding details: Use a permanent marker or paint pen to draw over transferred detail lines, or freehand details onto project.

Dry Brush: Do not dip brush in water. Dip a stipple brush or old paintbrush in paint; wipe most of the paint off onto a dry paper towel. Lightly rub the brush across the area to receive color. Repeat as needed for desired coverage of color.

Shading and highlighting: Dip one corner of a flat brush in water; blot on a paper towel. Dip dry corner of brush into paint. Stroke brush back and forth on palette until there is a gradual change from paint to water in each brush stroke. Stroke paint-loaded side of brush along detail line on project, pulling brush toward you and turning project if necessary. For shading, side load brush with a darker color of paint. For highlighting, side load brush with a lighter color of paint.

Spatter Painting: Dip the bristle tips of a dry toothbrush into paint, blot on a paper towel to remove excess, then pull thumb across bristles to spatter paint on project.

Sponge Painting: Use an assembly-line method when making several sponge-painted projects. Place project on a covered work surface. Practice sponge-painting technique on scrap paper until desired look is achieved. Paint projects with first color and allow to dry before moving to next color. Use a clean sponge for each additional color.

For allover designs, dab a dampened sponge piece (natural, compressed or household sponge) into paint; remove excess paint on a paper towel. Use a light stamping motion to paint item.

For painting with sponge shapes, dip a dampened sponge shape into paint; remove excess paint on a paper towel. Lightly press sponge shape onto project. Carefully lift sponge. For a reverse design, turn sponge shape over.

STENCILING

These instructions are written for multicolor stencils. For single-color stencils, make one stencil for entire design.

1. For first stencil, cut a piece from stencil plastic 1" larger than entire pattern. Center plastic over pattern and use a permanent pen to trace outlines of all areas of first color in stencil cutting key. For placement guidelines, outline remaining colored area using dashed lines. Using a new piece of plastic for each additional color in stencil cutting key, repeat for remaining stencils.

2. Place each plastic piece on cutting mat and use craft knife to cut out stencil along solid lines, making sure edges are smooth.

3. Hold or tape stencil in place. Using a clean, dry stencil brush or sponge piece, dip brush or sponge in paint. Remove excess paint on a paper towel. Brush or sponge should be almost dry to produce best results. Beginning at edge of cut-out area, apply paint in a stamping motion over stencil. If desired, highlight or shade design by stamping a lighter or darker shade of paint in cut-out area. Repeat until all of first stencil have been painted. Carefully remove stencil and allow paint to dry.

4. Using stencils in order indicated in color key and matching guidelines on stencils to previously stenciled area, repeat Step 3 for remaining stencils.

DECOUPAGE

1. Cut desired motifs from fabric or paper.

2. Apply decoupage glue to wrong sides of motifs.

3. Arrange motifs on project as desired; overlap as necessary for complete coverage. Smooth in place and allow to dry.

4. Allowing to dry after each application, apply 2 to 3 coats of clear acrylic sealer to project.

LETTERING

For unique and personal labels or lettering on your crafts, try using one of your favorite fonts from your computer...try the "bold" and "italic" buttons for different variations of the font. Size your words to fit your project, then print them out.

Using your printout as the pattern, use transfer paper to transfer the words to your project. If you're making appliqué letters, you'll need to trace the letters, in reverse, onto the paper side of the fusible web.

Don't forget about the old reliable lettering stencils...they're easy to use and come in a wide variety of styles and sizes. And, if you're already into memory page making, you probably have an alphabet set or 2 of rubber stamps...just select an inkpad type suitable for your project. Then, there are 100's of sizes, colors and shapes of sticker and rub-on letters...small, fat, shiny, flat, puffy, velvety, slick, smooth, rough...you get the idea! Only your imagination limits you.

DECORATED JAR LABELS
(shown on page 110)

GIFT WRAP & TAG IDEAS
(shown on page 105)

Nuts about You!

Home Made by

NEW YEAR'S EVE KIT
(shown on page 117)

Happy New Year!

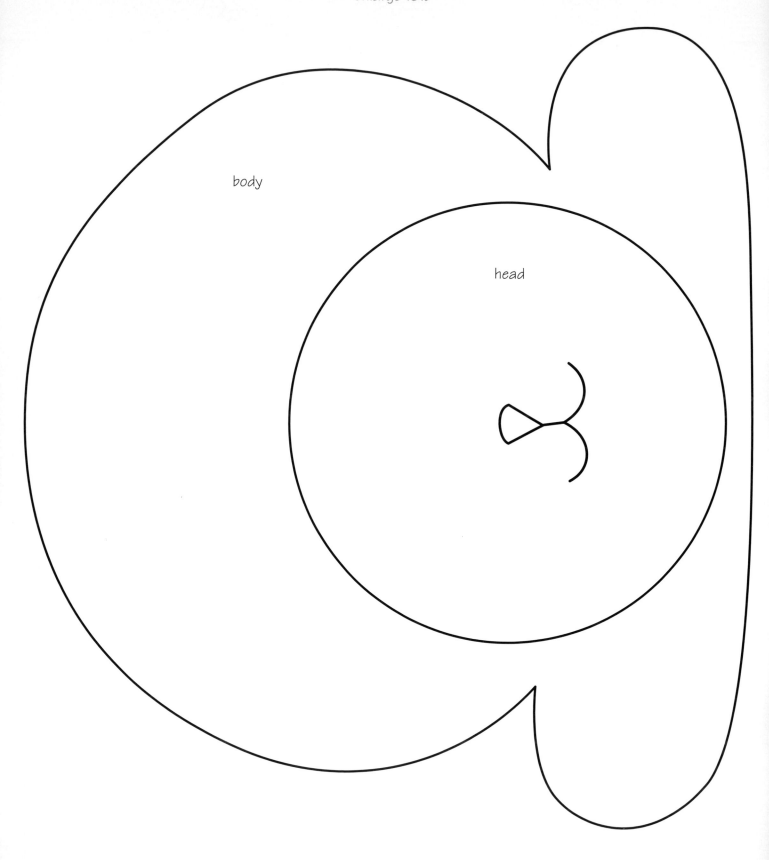

body

head

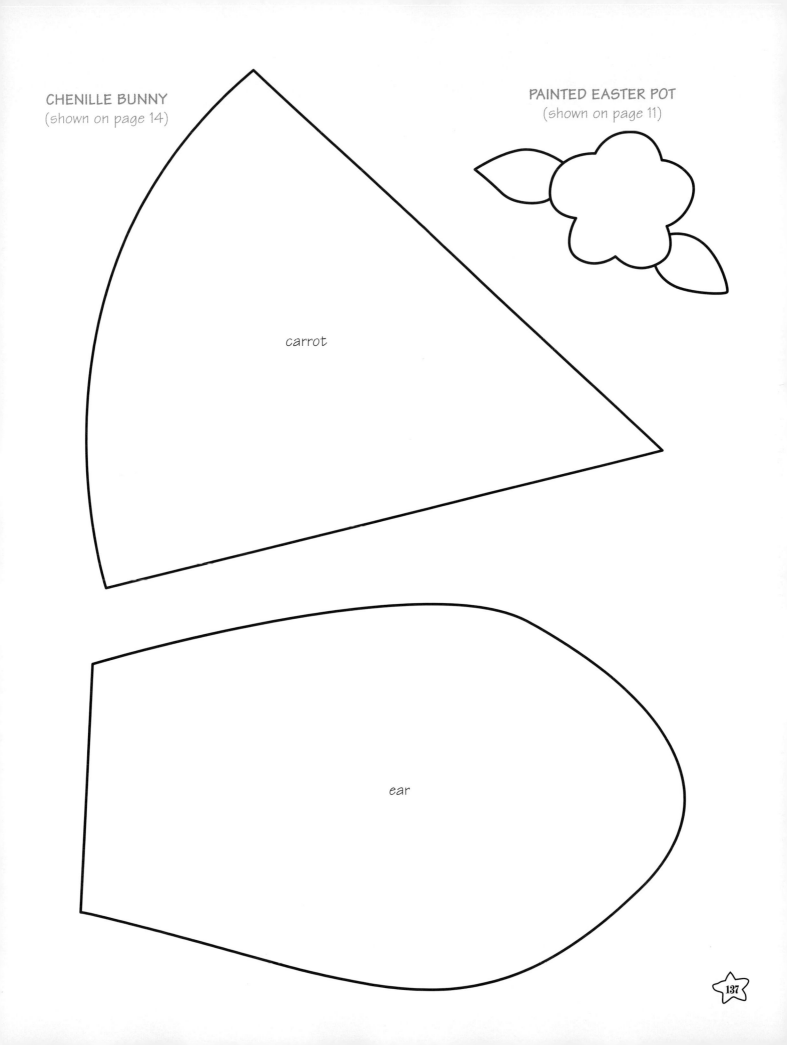

carrot

ear

EMBROIDERED PIN
(shown on page 14)

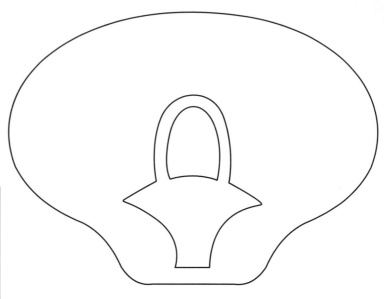

STITCHING KEY

FRIENDSHIP FLOWERS
(shown on page 21)

B

C

some **Seeds**
from my garden
to grow in yours!

V A R I e T Y :

A

Gooseberry Patch and Leisure Arts, Inc., grant permission to the owner of
this book to photocopy the designs on this page for personal use only.

SOOTHING TEA SET
(shown on page 29)

WASHTUB OF FLOWERS
(shown on page 25)

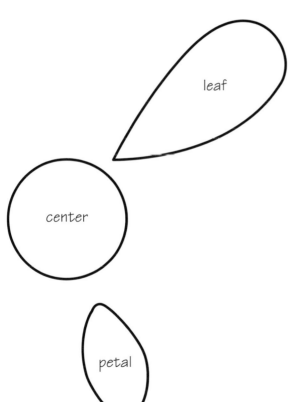

leaf

center

petal

More than anything,
I must have flowers,
always . . . . .

SPONGE-PAINTED
TABLECLOTH & FLOWERPOTS
(shown on page 44)

TEACHER'S VEST
(shown on page 69)

APPLE PENCILS KIDS
CRAYONS GLUE
STARS

64w x 43h

If friends were flowers I'd pick you

CROSS STITCHED BOUQUET

X	DMC	¼X	B'ST
♡	210		
⊖	309		
4	334	◨	◪
★	550		◪
‖	553		
▲	561	◨	
✔	562	◨	
▽	3325	◨	
◿	3753		
○	3822		
●	550 French Knot		

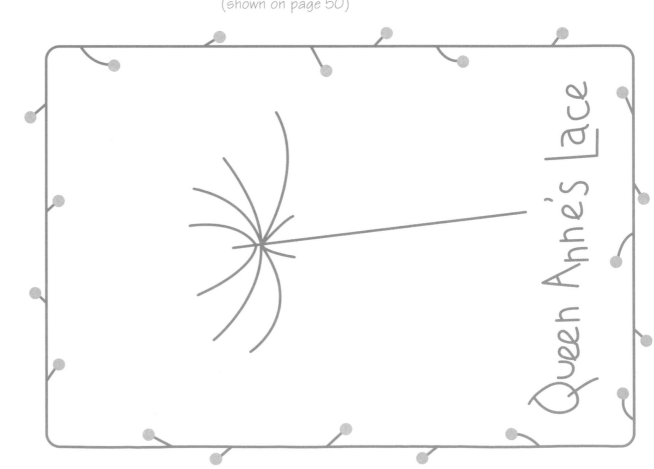

Queen Anne's Lace

STITCHING KEY

Gold = French Knots   *Green* = Backstitches
Blue = Blanket Stitch   **Pink** = Straight Stitches

142

thistle

Sunflowers

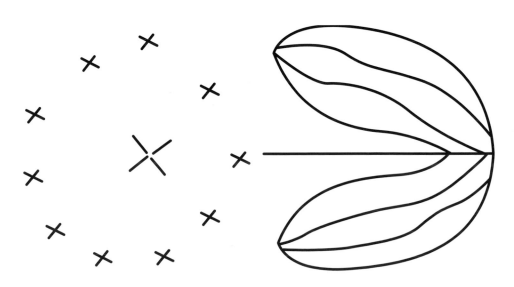

X = button placement

Cheery Cherry Apron
(shown on page 53)

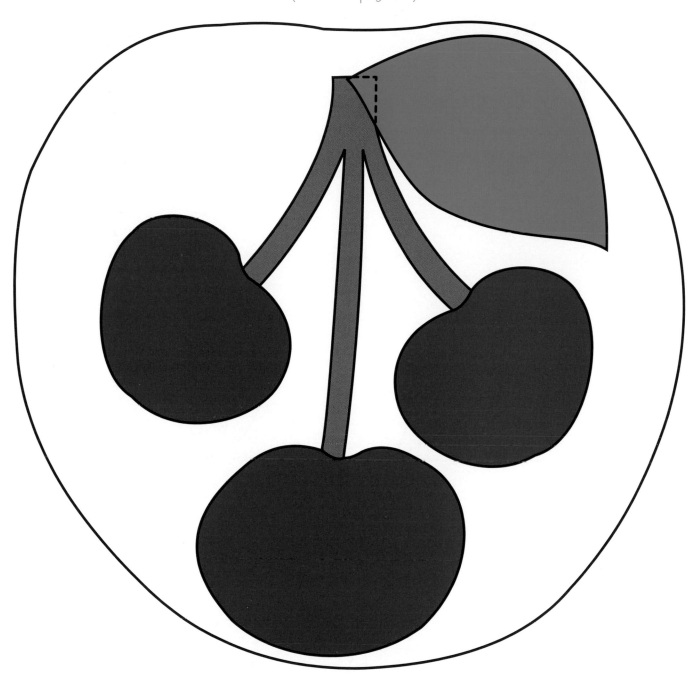

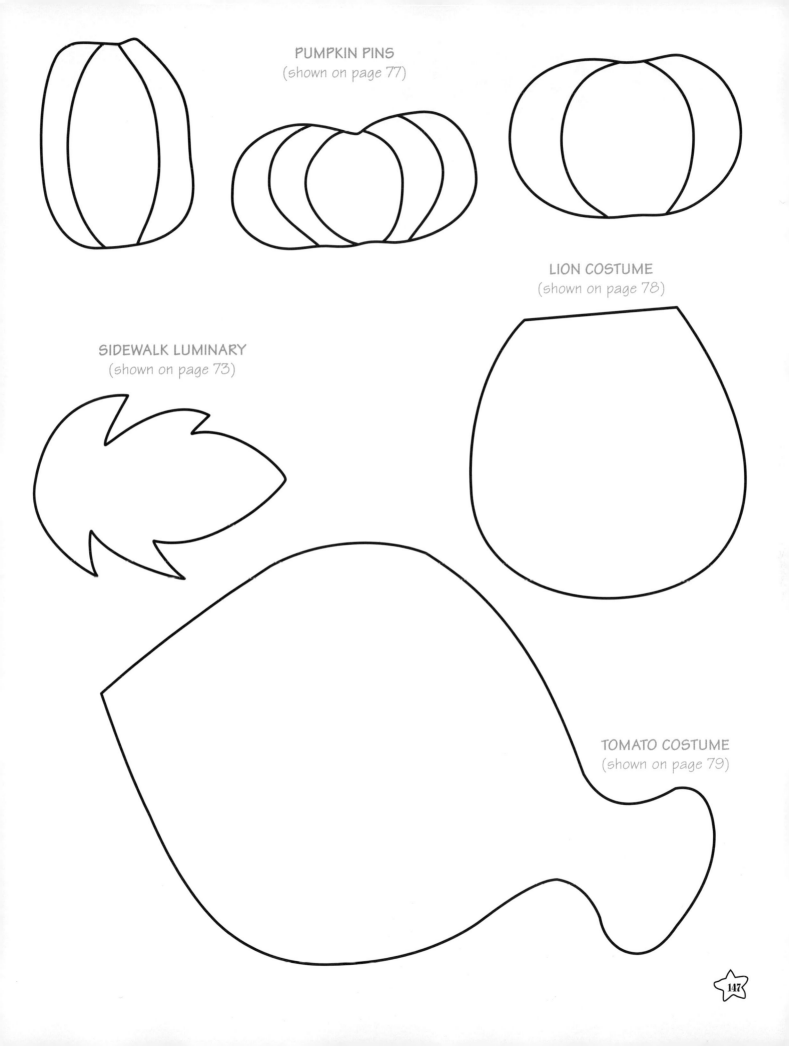

PUMPKIN PINS
(shown on page 77)

LION COSTUME
(shown on page 78)

SIDEWALK LUMINARY
(shown on page 73)

TOMATO COSTUME
(shown on page 79)

147

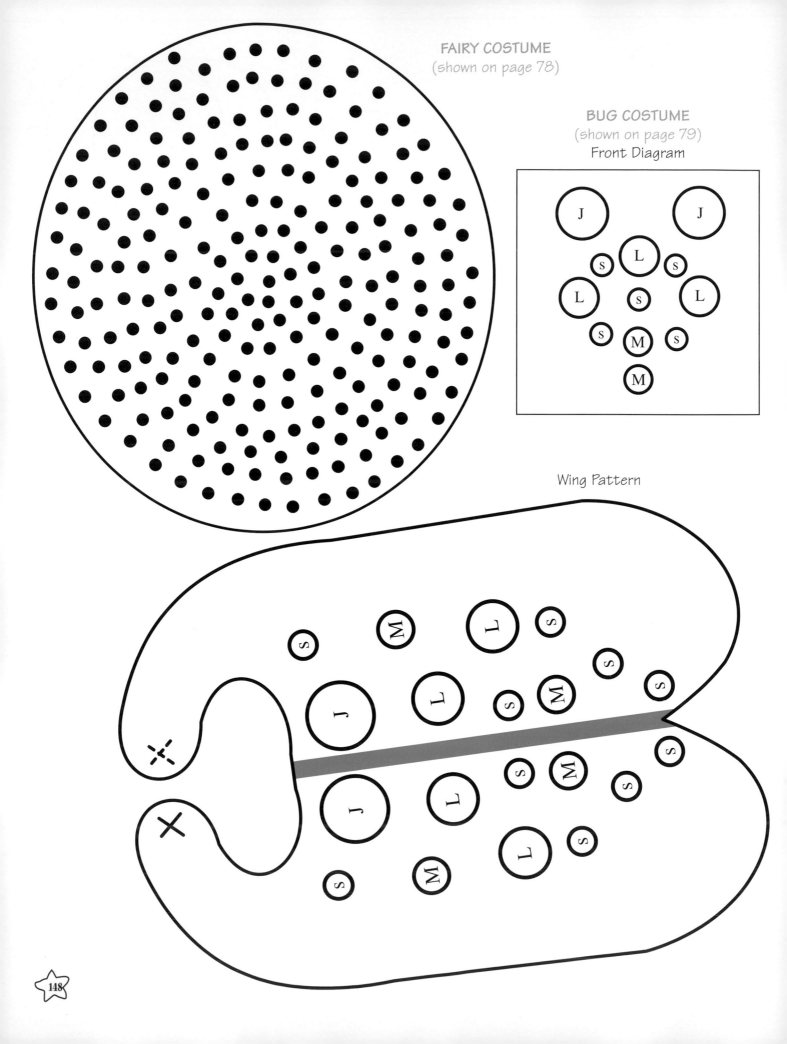

FAIRY COSTUME
(shown on page 78)

BUG COSTUME
(shown on page 79)
Front Diagram

Wing Pattern

"BOO" WELCOME MAT
(shown on page 75)

STITCHED BREAD CLOTH
(shown on page 87)

PAINTED TREAT POTS
(shown on page 81)

STAMPED TREAT BAGS
(shown on page 81)

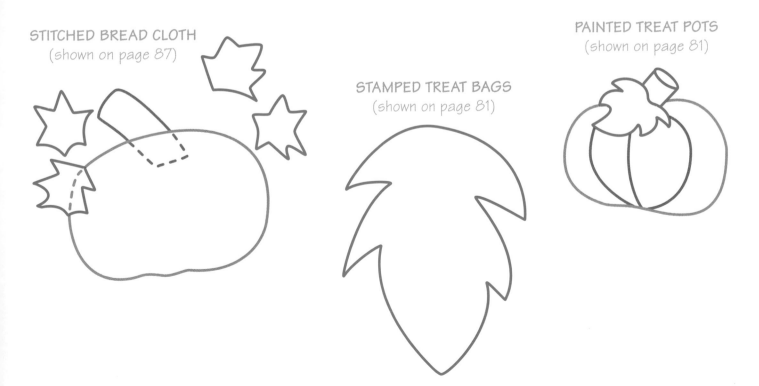

To give thanks is good

150

LEAF PLACEMAT
(shown on page 87)
(enlarge 125%)

"THANKS" WALL HANGING
(shown on page 86)

COLLECTOR'S SHELF
(shown on page 92)

COOKIE EXCHANGE INVITATIONS
(shown on page 101)
GINGERBREAD MAN TREAT BAGS
(shown on page 103)

OLD-FASHIONED ORNAMENTS
(shown on page 107)

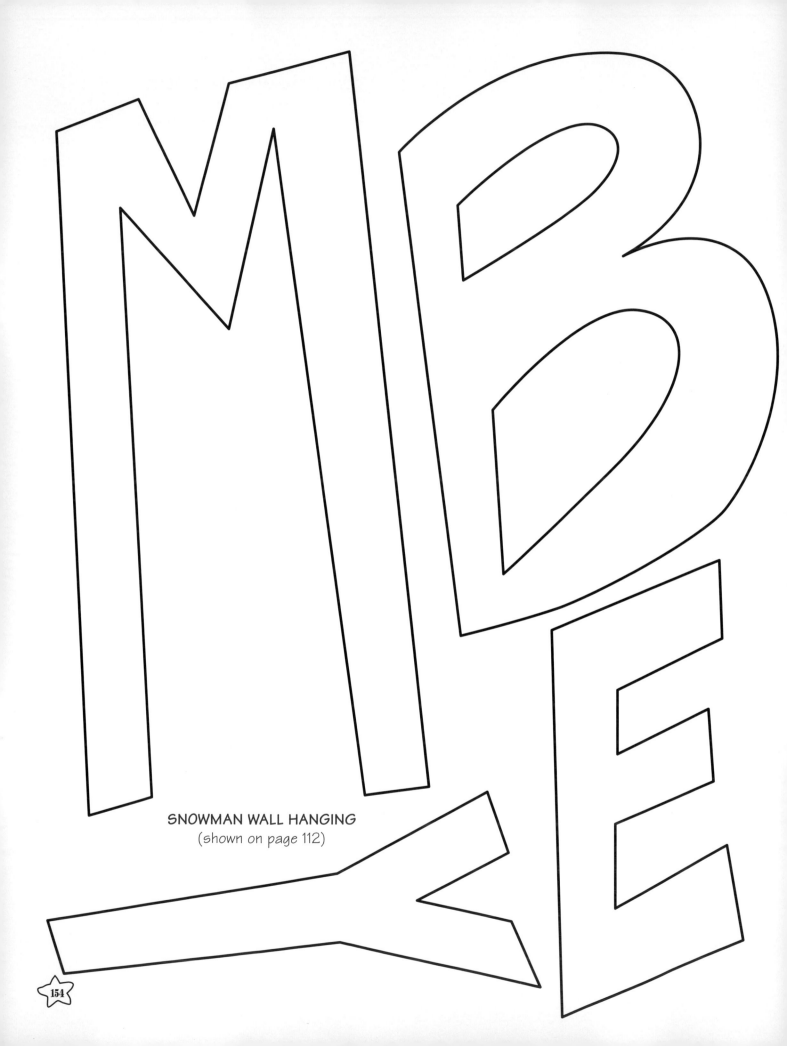

SNOWMAN WALL HANGING
(shown on page 112)

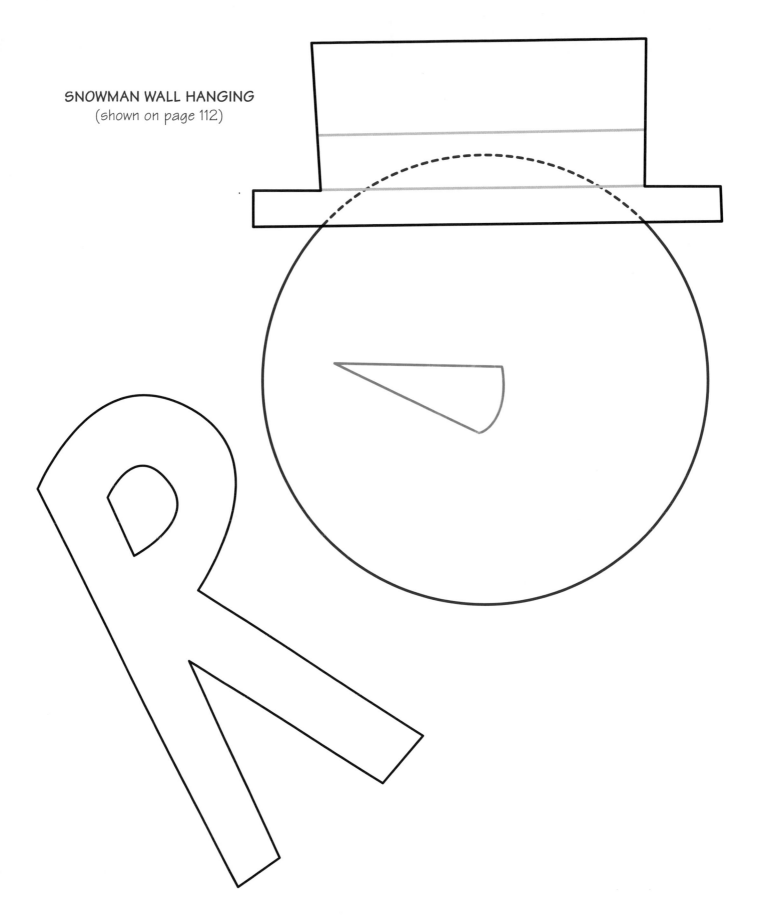

SNOWMAN WALL HANGING
(shown on page 112)

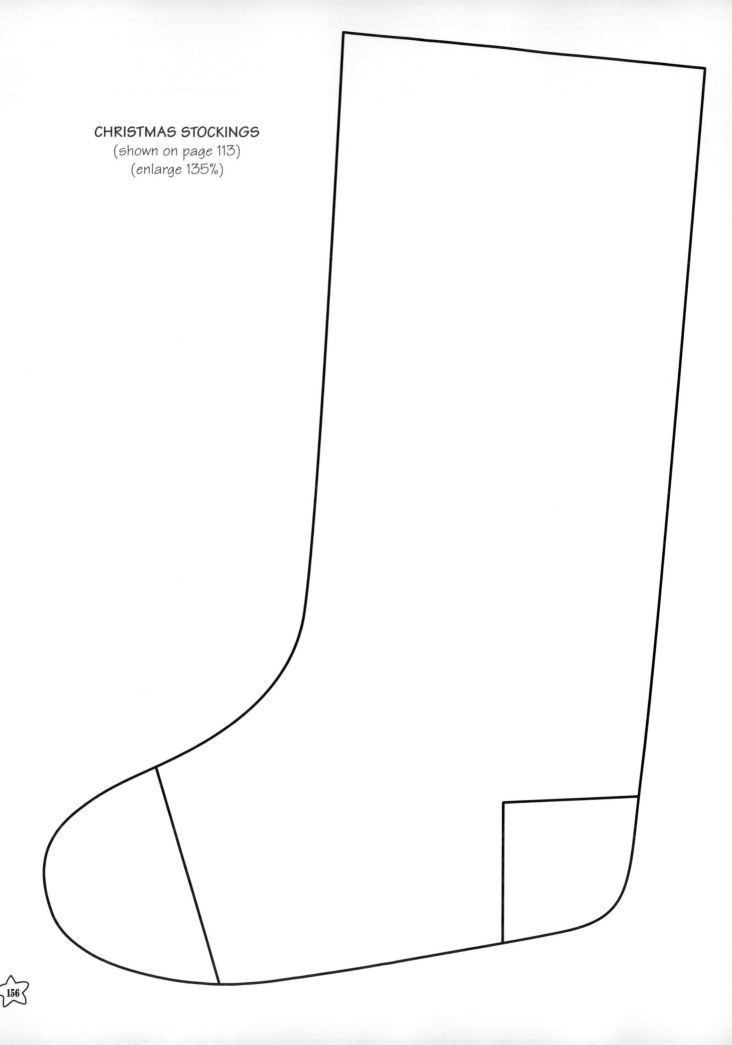

CHRISTMAS STOCKINGS
(shown on page 113)
(enlarge 135%)

156

WINDOW TO MY HEART CARD
(shown on page 120)

QUILT PIECE ANGEL
(shown on page 114)

157

PROJECT INDEX

RECIPE INDEX

Credits

We want to extend a warm thank you to the people who allowed us to photograph some of our projects at their homes: Joan Adams, Sandra Cook, Thomas Hankins, Brenda Hogan, the Kymer family, Beth Morgan, Ellison Poe, Nancy Gunn Porter, Catherine Smith, Becky Thompson, Leighton Weeks and the Westerguard family. We especially want to thank Cindy George for allowing us to photograph our section introductions at her home.

To Chris Olsen, we extend a special word of thanks for creating the beautiful front porch décor shown on pages 8-9, 38-39, 66-67 and 90-91. Chris is a talented landscape designer, and the owner of Horticare Landscape Management Company, Inc., of Little Rock, Arkansas.

Our sincere thanks also goes to The Good Earth Garden Center and Nurseries of Little Rock, Arkansas, for providing many of the beautiful plants shown in our photographs.

We want to especially thank photographers Ken West of The Peerless Group, Jerry R. Davis of Jerry Davis Photography and Andrew Uilkie of Uilkie Photography, all of Little Rock, Arkansas, for their excellent work. Photography stylists Sondra Harrison Daniel, Karen Smart Hall and Charlisa Erwin Parker also deserve a special mention for the high quality of their collaboration with the photographers.

We extend a special word of thanks to Terrece Beesley, who designed the *Cross-Stitched Bouquet* shown on page 33; Mary Ayres, who designed the *Framed Stitched Pieces* and *Embroidered Pillows* shown on page 50; Judy Patterson, who designed the *Pumpkin Pins* shown on page 77; and Kathie Rueger, who designed the *Collector's Shelf* shown on page 92.

We would like to recognize Viking Husqvarna Sewing Machine Company of Cleveland, Ohio, for providing the sewing machines used to make many of our projects, and Design Master Color Tool, Inc., of Boulder, Colorado, for providing the wood-tone spray used on some of our projects. We also thank East Side Mouldings of Lititz, Pennsylvania, for providing the moulding used for the *"Thanks" Wall Hanging* shown on page 86.

A special word of thanks to Karla Edgar, Kathy Elrod, Rose Glass Klein, Jo Nortier, Glenda Taylor and Nora Faye Taylor for assisting with making and testing many of the projects and recipes in this book.

All's well that ends well. ~old adage